Given

by the

Lincoln Christian College

Alumni Association

As Part

of a

$100,000 Gift,

1968-1971

Christianity
and
Classical Civilization

Christianity
and
Classical Civilization

by

RALPH STOB, Ph.D.

Professor of Classical Languages
Calvin College, Grand Rapids, Mich.

WM. B. EERDMANS PUBLISHING COMPANY

Grand Rapids   1950   Michigan

CHRISTIANITY AND CLASSICAL CIVILIZATION
by Ralph Stob, Ph.D.

Set up and printed, September, 1950

Preface

THE SUBJECT treated in the following pages has engaged my thought and part of my time over a period of years. That is due, in the first place, to the nature of the question itself. Every thinking Christian will necessarily ask some questions about the origin of his beliefs, about how that which is declared and proclaimed as the Truth in the Word, stood in relation to the pagan world in which it was first made known. But the Christian scholar will face the questions of environment and environmental relationships much more consciously and consistently. And he who has as his special field of study and teaching the classics of Greece and Rome will be compelled to do so. As soon as he gets beyond mere grammar and the teaching of the language as a mere tool, and aims at an understanding and evaluation of the ideas expressed, as soon as he goes beyond form to content, he becomes acutely aware of the question of relationships and comparative values.

During the last half century and more much study has been made and countless books have been written on the subject. Especially liberal Christianity has interested itself in environmental factors as to the origin of Christianity. That is one of its real achievements, as well as one of its real weaknesses. For it has made too much of environmental factors, of historical antecedents, attempting to explain all thereby. On the other hand, conservative or orthodox Christianity has made too little of the same, putting Christianity in a sealed compartment. As a result one meets with most conflicting views. Hence both the intrinsic importance of the subject and the contradictory views propounded have contributed to the investigation of the subject.

Likewise, they have determined something about the form in which the material is presented. The attempt has been to make it intelligible to others than the experts. That aim explains why many direct quotations are made in full, instead of a reference to the passage.

A word as to the bibliography. It is rather extensive but by no means exhaustive. In the main books have been listed to which reference was made in the text.

Finally, my thanks are due to some of my colleagues with whom discussions have been carried on with reference to the problem. Special thanks is given to my colleague Dr. William T. Radius of the Latin Department, who also has read a good part of the manuscript. However, I alone am to be held responsible for the views expressed.

Ralph Stob

Calvin College,
Grand Rapids, Michigan,
September 1, 1950

Table of Contents

Christianity
and
Classical Civilization

CHAPTER I

Introduction

ON EVERY HAND the statement is made that we are living
in a complex world. The statement is entirely correct. The
smallest item of our lives is conditioned by a host of other
items and forces. It is difficult to isolate anything and look at
it by itself. That brings about the perplexity and the conflict
of opinion about life.

There is however, another complexity in life of which men
are not so cognizant. Not only is our life now conditioned by
various forces, but the life itself is complex in that two rivers
have emptied themselves into the stream of modern civilization. The origins of our present civilization are varied and in
contrast, so that in the mingling they have a strange mixture.

We must see our life as a present one but also, to understand
it, we must trace our present civilization to its sources. The
backward trail is a long one. Back through the centuries we
must go. For our American civilization began by being im-
ported from Europe. And whence European culture? That, in
turn, is the product of centuries in which the church had great
influence. Everywhere the church has left its mark. To the
peoples of Europe was brought the gospel with its high ideals
of human life.

But that Christianity did not come to barbarous peoples.
Behind the advent of Christian teaching lay another civilization. Before the soldiers of the Cross in the church militant
had brought their messages to the peoples of Western Europe,
the hosts of Roman legions had marched into every hamlet
and land. The Roman eagle had spread his wings so that all
the countries of Western Europe and the Near East were

under his sway. Following the army came the penetration of Roman ideas into the vast territory of Europe.

But behind Rome lies another force. The civilization which Rome attained was largely an importation from still further east. Little Greece had risen to unprecedented heights in civilization and Rome had taken over its accomplishments. Preceding the grandeur that was Rome, the glory that was Greece had reached its zenith. Thus from little Greece comes in the main the one river which empties itself in the stream of modern life.

It winds itself into the towns and villages and cities of Italy. Slowly it penetrates Roman life, and the result is Graeco-Roman civilization. Into the stream of that pagan life came the waters of life through the preaching especially of St. Paul. Slowly the leaven works. Rome and the empire have seen their best days. There was disintegration from within, but working too is the gospel of Jesus Christ which slowly but surely is weakening that life of pagan antiquity. A marvelous chapter of history is being written. Christianity comes out triumphant. Then for some centuries the church has full sway. Paganism has succumbed and Christianity rules.

Has the civilization of Greece and Rome entirely disappeared? For a time apparently, for the Ages are Dark. But there comes a time when another glorious chapter of human history is written. Slowly there comes the Revival of Learning, when the volumes of Greece and Rome are again discovered. Men assiduously read and study what those heroes of old have said. The Renaissance blossoms forth and ever since the civilization of Greece and Rome has found a permanent home in Western civilization.

These two are the rivers of the modern world. Christianity, the gospel of Jesus Christ, and the civilization of Greece and Rome make up the river. Such is in broad lines the fundamental, underlying complexity of our civilization. Is it Christian? Is it pagan? Which is dominant? Or are the two streams carriers of the same pure waters of life?

The problem then is the relation between these two. Anyone who has reflected for a moment on the matter will readily agree that it is both a significant and a tremendous question. Face it one must because in the fullness of time God sent forth His Son, born of a woman, born under the law. What does it mean that the time was full? Or if one uses other words in what sense was the world ripe for the Advent? For it is not sufficient merely to assert that he came in the fullness of time. Surely that means that He came into the flesh at a divinely appointed time. But just as surely that means that there was something proper, fitting, propitious about that moment. For God in His wisdom does nothing arbitrarily. There is something in the historical set-up which makes that the proper moment for the Advent. It just could not have taken place a thousand years earlier nor later. What then are the factors and the elements which make that the propitious moment? To answer that implies a knowledge of the world of the New Testament. But, standing on the basis of the Word, it means much more than a knowledge of a host of facts and phenomena. There is implied a philosophy of history. The divine eye canvassing all the phenomena which the divine hand has caused to be determines that just then and at no other time shall His own Son be sent into the world with the gospel. It is our task then to seek to discover the divine plan and wisdom in the histories of the peoples immediately involved in the Advent of the Son of God and the coming of the full truth through Him. All the events must be looked at from above to learn something of the marvelous revelation of the plan of God. Again one may speak of the preparation for Christianity. With some the term is taboo. So one must set himself to ask in what way, through the particular phenomena of the world in its history, there was a preparation for the Advent. Even among the gentiles God had not left himself without witness. There too is a revelation of God. But it is different from that among His chosen ones. What then is the relation between general and special revelation? No general statement that the special complements and corrects the general is sufficient. To see the divine plan in its beauty one must get a clear view of particular bits of revealed truth in the attitudes, outlooks, utterances, institutions and practices of the pagan peoples. But again one must see wherein that revelation, even at its best, fell short of the full truth of special revelation. One must see then the real complement or corrective in special revelation. That becomes a fascinating but also a laborious task. But nothing short of that will suffice. There is in the world of the New Testament not only evidence of special grace operating in the hearts and lives of men, but also of a common grace to all. What then is the content of each, and what is the relation between the two?

The object of this study is therefore twofold. There is the phase of an historical investigation as to the nature of the relation of original or primitive Christianity as incorporated in the Scripture and the pagan culture of Greece and Rome which preceded it, and into whose world the new religion came. That study is worthwhile in itself because of the very divergent views which have been held with reference to the question. But it is not merely an historical investigation. For "within Christian history itself there is a constant interaction of the Hebrew and Hellenic principles which together make the main sources of our culture."[1] And that interaction has been of such a character that at times the Hebrew view has been engulfed by the Greek. It is the conviction of the author that the present age is one which is much more Hellenic than Christian. Within the Christian church much of purely pagan thought has supplanted the Scripture teaching. When many modern, so-called liberal views propounded and accepted in the church are examined, they reveal themselves as being substantially identical with those of pagan antiquity. And the deeply tragical thing is that

---

1. Berdyaev, N.: The Meaning of History p. 106.

men are being urged to accept these views as being really Christian, while in reality they are in conflict with or an outright denial of the teachings of Scripture. Hence this study aims to point out something of the real character of modernism as it has entered into and gained the upper hand in many denominations.

CHAPTER II

Christianity and Paganism

A. *Views Held in the Early Church*

IN THE INTRODUCTION it was stated that the stream of modern civilization goes back to two sources, the one Graeco-Roman and the other Christian. At the outset then a fair question would be whether these two are in any definite relation to each other. How must we conceive of them? Are the two mutually exclusive in character? Are they in contrast and in conflict on all points? Has Christianity nothing in common with the world into which it came? Is it altogether and entirely antithetical? Or must one think of it as a complement? Is Christianity a mere addition to what was already present? Or is there something unique about it so that it stands out by contrast? And if there is something unique, something distinctive, something peculiar to Christian teaching, then still the questions are numerous. Immediately the question presents itself whether these differences and similarities go to the heart of the matter. For it can very well be that there are many differences but that they all are surface differences. Instead of reaching the core of Christianity they may lie far in the periphery. Hence the differences may be superficial, while at bottom there is agreement. And so the questions multiply.

To answer these questions implies a great deal. No intelligent answer can be given unless very definite assumptions are made, or rather, unless certain requirements are met. How can an answer be given unless there be a fairly definite and adequate knowledge of both? He who knows only the classics of Greece and Rome cannot be trusted to give the answer. Nor is he who knows only the New Testament able to give the answer. What is required is that the individual have a genuine knowledge of both. He must know and love the teachings of both the New Testament and the writings and the institutions of Greece and Rome. Again, there is need for a penetration into the real meaning and attitude of both. What is implied is that the individual have a comprehensive and fundamental grasp on Christianity so that he has an insight into its basic considerations and assumptions. Not merely a knowledge of and ability to quote Scripture passages is necessary, but a rounded and deep interpretation of the passages in relation to the whole of Scripture. And again the same is essential for the other field. Not merely an aesthetic appreciation of the beauties of Greek and Latin literature. Nor the ability to quote aptly from Euripides, Sophocles, or Plato, Cicero or Horace, but a genuine knowledge of the underlying trends of the teaching of the Greeks and Romans, so that the true picture is seen with the necessary shadows and lights. In brief, a philosophical grasp of the striving and ideals of the pagan soul as it expressed itself in the wealth of literary forms, the poetry, the philosophy, the history, the drama, and also the ethics, the art, and the religion. There must be an attempt at the right evaluation of all these, so that the genius of the people is known.

Any one can readily see that this is a great task. Fortunately one does need to begin from the bottom up. The two have so long been the subject of earnest investigation and appraisal that a wealth of material is at hand. At the same time it must be sifted and weighed very carefully and even then the author is certain that the conclusions arrived at will not be shared by nor be acceptable to all.

The real relation between Christianity and the paganism of antiquity has been frequently investigated. And nearly as frequent as are the investigations, as varied are the answers. The variety, of course, is due to a lack of a full understanding of either Graeco-Roman civilization, or of Christianity, or of both. It has been, and still is, so easy to center the attention on a minor detail and then to declare that the two are in full agreement or at absolute variance.

The question of the relation of the two was faced very early in the Christian Church and by the Pagan world into which it came. Strange creatures, these Christians! What were they like anyway? Peculiar people, to be sure. But where did they get their peculiar ideas? And how far would they go in defense of them? Many at first thought that they were a branch of the Jews. Naturally such a view would find support. The religion had originated in Palestine, its founder was a Jew, and the early disciples were also. Paul, the chief apostle, was a Jew, and he first visited the synagogues in every locality. But soon it was discovered that the Jews generally hated the founder of the new religion and hated Paul and the followers of Jesus. These Christians were eyed with suspicion by the pagans, and with hatred by the Jews. Thus in the minds of the people the thought took shape that there was a "third" people. Thus far it had been Jew and Gentile or barbarian, but now the Christian arose as a third class. Whence did these people get their peculiar ideas and practices?

Really, the thing that disturbed the Roman government, was not the ideas but the practices of these Christians. You couldn't drag them to the amphitheatre to watch the spectacles and to listen to the excited populace ever ready to demand something more sensational, something more stupendous, something more thrilling. At first the Christians would not serve in the army because by doing so they had to take an oath of allegiance which violated their conscientious fidelity to the Lord Jesus. Likewise they refused to participate in the devotions to the gods and goddesses of the empire. No wonder they were called atheists, for they had no images which were so characteristic of pagan religion. And in morals generally they revealed themselves as opposed to the current practices and as manifesting a love for the brethren which was above all expectation. Nothing like it had ever been seen by the pagans.

Whence then did they get such ideas? That was the question asked by their adversaries. But not only the adversaries were faced by this question. The Christians themselves had to give an answer. As soon as Christianity became of any considerable influence, the saints were put on the defensive to declare the origin of their beliefs and practices. Thus arose the apologists of the Christian faith. Repeatedly the two ideas of the character and the origin of the Christian beliefs are put side by side. They made comparison of the ideas of Christianity and paganism. When differences or similarities appeared an explanation had to be found, and various explanations were given.

To the examination of these similarities and these explanations by the Christians we must now turn. Generally speaking there were four ways of accounting for the phenomena of similarity and difference between Christian teaching and that of the pagans. For it was recognized that there were great perversions of the truth and morality, but also that there were many noble sentiments.[1] To account for these noble sentiments which approximated the Christian view, recourse was taken to some very peculiar explanations.

The first explanation saw practically nothing but evil in the pagan world. The ideals and practices were regarded as extremely perverse, as opposed to all the good and the true in the Christian religion. The emphasis is laid on the contrast and the conflict between the two. A different and contrary spirit pervades the two movements. The world of paganism is under the direct control and influence of Satan and the world of demons. It is thru these demons who inspired the ancients that wicked perversions and imitations of the true view of God, man, and morality entered into the world. The world was dominated by the evil Spirit, who controlled the minds even of the noblest of antiquity. Briefly, it can be said that Chris-

---

1. Heinrici, C. F.: Hellenismus and Christentum, p. 4.

tianity was regarded as the direct denial of and antithesis of all that had gone before. Especially hostile to the heathen philosophy were Tatian, Theophilus, Tertullian, and the author of the Epistle to Diognetus. A quotation from Tertullian will indicate the attitude quite sufficiently: "What in common have Athens and Jerusalem? The Academy and the Church? Heretics and Christians? Let them see to it who teach a stoical and Platonic and dialectic Christianity."[2] And Justin Martyr is explicit on this influence of evil spirits. He writes, "and we proceed to demonstrate that they have been uttered by the influence of wicked demons, to deceive and lead astray the human race."[3]

The second explanation which agrees with and may have been taken from the Jewish writings[4] might be regarded as a variation of the first. For it too lays emphasis on the part which the spiritual beings have played but the manner in which it is done is emphasized. And, indeed it is a curious explanation. Recourse is taken to the passage in Scripture in which, "the sons of God saw the daughters of men that they were fair; and they took them wives of all which they chose."[5] The explanation then is that the angels married the daughters of men and in that relation revealed many of the truths to their wives who transmitted it to their offspring so that it became the common heritage of their posterity. So Tertullian writes: "For when to an age (much more ignorant than ours) they (the angels who rushed from heaven to the daughters of men) had disclosed certain well-concealed substances, and several not well-revealed arts."[6] This view found favor among a number of the defenders of the faith,[7] and is described in a very humorous way by Lecky in the following words: "For the angels who had been fascinated by the antedeluvian ladies,

2. De Praescriptionibus adversus Hereticos VII; cf. X.
3. I Apology LIV.
4. Book of Jubliees 5:1; Book of Enoch 6:1; Secrets of Enoch 18:4-5.
5. Gen. 6:2.
6. On female Dress, I, chap. 2; cf. Veiling of Virgins VII.
7. Clement of Alexandria: Strom. V chap. 1; cf. Lactantius Vol. I, p. 127.

had endeavored to ingratiate themselves with their fair companions by giving them an abstract of the metaphysical learning which was then current in heaven, and the substance of these conversations, being transmitted by traditions, supplied the pagan philosophers with their leading notions."[8]

A third explanation is that of direct borrowing. Arguments are presented repeatedly to show that Israel was a more ancient people than the Greeks, and the conclusion is drawn that since the Greeks are later in time the writings of the Israelites were known to them and were used by them. Hence the similarity in teaching. The one example most frequently given is that of Moses and Plato. Plato in his travels in Egypt had become acquainted with the books of Moses and the noble ideas and sentiments in Plato find their source there. Plato is guilty in some instances of plagiarism, and in others of having taken the idea from a writer of the Old Testament.

It is well to give a few examples since this explanation is found much more frequently than the two preceding. So we read: "Pythagoras, who expounded the doctrines of his own philosophy mystically by means of symbols, himself seems to have entertained thoughts about the unity of God not unworthy of his residence in Egypt."[9]

At times it appears that all the good in various phases of Greek life owes its existence to this source. Thus Justin Martyr writes: "For whatever the lawgivers or philosophers uttered well, they elaborated by finding and contemplating some aspect of the Word. But since they did not know the whole of the Word, which is Christ, they often contradicted themselves.[10] Though this passage is capable of an interpretation of the Word which would not mean the written Word, in another passage Justin does refer to the written Word. For we read, "Orpheus and Homer, and Solon who wrote the laws

---

8. Lecky, Wm.: History of European Morals Vol. I p. 344.
9. Justin Martyr: Address to the Greeks XIX.
10 idem: II Apology X.

of the Athenians, and Pythagoras, and Plato, and some others, when they had been in Egypt, and had taken advantage of the history of Moses."[11]

The references to Plato's being influenced by and borrowing from Moses are numerous. I shall mention only a few. Justin Martyr writes: "And the physiological discussion concerning the Son of God in the Timaeus of Plato where he says 'He placed him cross-wise in the universe' he borrowed in like manner from Moses."[12] Again "And that you may learn that it was from our teachers that Plato borrowed that statement that God, having altered matter which was shapeless, made the world, hear the words spoken thru Moses, who, as was shown, was the first prophet, and of greater antiquity than Greek writers."[13] I have given a few examples from Justin but the same idea is found in a number of the defenders of the faith.[14]

Before we pass on to the last explanation we should take note that the early opponents of Christianity used this same argument of borrowing. Naturally they reversed the process. Instead of Plato having stolen from Moses, it is now presented that all the Christian teachings were borrowed from Greek mythology and literature. Much of Celsus' argument against Christianity rests on this pivotal point. According to him the Tower of Babel account is a perversion of the story of Aloeus (Odyssey XI) and the destruction of Sodom of the story of

11. idem: Address to the Greeks XIV; cf. XXIV, XXVIII.
12. idem: I Apology LX.
13. idem: I Apology LIX, cf. XLIV; cf. Hortatory Address to the Greeks XX, XXII, XXV, XXVI, XXIX, XXX,XXXI, XXXIII.
14. Clement of Alexandria: Strom. I, chap. I, XVIII, XXV.; idem II, chap. I, V.; idem V., chap. I, XI, XIVff.
Clement of Alexandria: Exhortation to the Greeks VI, 60.
Clement of Alexandria: Paedagogus I, chap. VIII.; idem II, chap. X.
Origen: Contra Celsum VI, chap. XIX; idem VII, chap. XXX.
Origen: De Principiis III, chap. VI.
Tatian: Address to the Greeks XL.
Theophilus: Epistle to Autolycus I, chap. XIV.; idem II, chap. XXXVII.
Tertullian: Apologeticus 47.
Tertullian: On Soul's Testimony Vol. III, p. 178.
Eusebius: Preparation for the Gospel 298d, 460c, 507d.

Phaethon.[15] The story of the flood is a perversion of that of Deucalion.[16] The teaching of Jesus on the turning of the other cheek originates with Plato in the Crito.[17] Thus Celsus goes on trying to prove that the Greeks had the original and the Israelites and the Christians stole from them.

The last explanation given by the apologists is that already suggested in the passage from Justin Martyr. According to it the ancients had some acquaintance with the Word. This, however, suggests too much to the modern reader who knows no Greek. Justin says that they found and contemplated some aspect of the Word. But word suggests to most readers the Scripture, and Justin does not necessarily have that in mind. The difficulty arises because Justin uses the word 'logos" which can be translated "Word," but is not to be taken in the sense of the written Word. The whole question of the meaning of logos will be taken up more fully later. Suffice it to say here that the emphasis is not put on the written or spoken word in logos, but rather it is regarded as an immanent something in the world. It is the element of reason, of thought, of idea, which lies in and behind the phenomena. It is the force which orders and guides the universe, present in the world itself. It is this logos which makes out of the world a cosmos, an ordered whole, instead of a chaos, an unordered, unsystematized mass.

It is this element of Reason, of Thought, which is present in all things, and hence also in man. Yes, it is in man that it fully comes to its own. At least man is distinguished through his having intelligence. Hence all men share in it, some more and others less. It is this reason or Logos in man which gives expression to ideas. Therefore, wherever these ideas have been expressed by men there will be some degree of similarity, because the same Logos is working in and through them all.

---

15. Origen: Contra Celsum IV, chap. XXI.
16. Origen: idem IV, chap. XLI.
17. Origen: idem VII, chap. LVIII.

It is therefore possible that Justin Martyr had this thought in mind in the passage to which reference has been made. Certainly it is not foreign to him. For we read, "For each man spoke well in proportion to the share he had of the spermatic word, seeing what was related to it. . . . For all writers were able to see realities darkly through the sowing of the implanted word that was in them."[18] Another quotation from Justin will illustrate the point sufficiently. He writes: "And those of the stoic school — since, so far as their moral teaching went, they were admirable, as were also the poets in some particulars, on account of the seed of reason (Logos) implanted in every race of men, were hated and put to death."[19]

The same view is held by others. In fact it is developed by them so that it becomes quite prominent in their views. Clement of Alexandria writes: "But all, in my opinion, are illuminated by the dawn of Light. Let all, therefore, both Greeks and barbarians, who have aspired after the truth — both those who possess not a little, and those who have any portion — produce whatever they have of the word of truth."[20]

It is interesting to note what use was made of this view by the apologists, though there is no agreement among them on this point. Some take a very moderate view and others a much more extreme one. The moderate one maintains that through the Logos present and operating in the pagans, many excellent statements were made, and genuine truths were advocated. At the same time they maintain that there is a great difference between this operation of the Logos, and the full manifestation of the Logos of God, Jesus Christ. The truths are shadowy, incomplete, at times contradictory and even subverted. They, however, do serve the general purpose of being preparatory to the perfect manifestation which was to come in the Christ.

---

18. Justin Martyr: II Apology XIII.
19. idem: IIApology VIII; cf. I Apology V; II Apology X.
20. Clement of Alexandria: Strom. I, chap. XIII; cf. I, chap. I; Origen: Contra Celsum VI, chap. III.

On this point Justin Martyr presents both views. We read: "For whatever either lawgivers or philosophers uttered well, they elaborated by finding and contemplating some part of the Word. But since they did not know the whole of the Word, which is Christ, they often contradicted themselves."[21] It is especially in Clement of Alexandria that we find the idea of a preparation for the Gospel through Greek philosophy. He admits the weakness in Greek philosophy in these words. "For each soul has its own proper nutriment; some growing by knowledge and science, and others feeding on the Hellenic philosophy, the whole of which, like nuts, is not eatable."[22] At the same time he sees its many fine teachings for he says. "For this was a schoolmaster to bring the Hellenic mind, as the law the Hebrews, to Christ. Philosophy, therefore, **was** a preparation, paving the way for him who is perfected in Christ."[23]

Justin at times identifies the manifestation of the logos in the pagans and in Christ to such an extent that he calls these pagans Christians. This is what was spoken of as the extreme view. He says, "and those who lived reasonably (i. e. with Logos) are Christians, even though they have been thought Atheists, as among the Greeks, Socrates and Heracleitus, and men like them."[24] He makes this explicit statement about Socrates: "For no one trusts in Socrates so as to die for his doctrine, but in Christ, who was partially known even by Socrates — for he was and is the Word who is in every man."[25]

These various interpretations by the Apologists have been given in the order of approximation to the correct view. As has become evident from the quotations the individual apologists do not restrict themselves to any one of the four. Naturally he who saw nothing but perversion and untruth in the

---

21. Justin Martyr: II Apology X.
22. Strom. I, chap. 1.
23. idem I, chap. V; cf. I, chap. XVI.
24. I Apology XLVI.
25. II Apology X; cf. I Apology V.

views of the pagan writers was inclined to either the first or
second interpretation. At the same time he might in some
other passage refer to the truth as having been borrowed from
the writers of the Old Testament. This is not necessarily a
real conflict for he would maintain that the ideas so far as
they originated with the pagan author were erroneous, and that
the good ideas had their source elsewhere.

The first three of these interpretations are entirely untenable. The first because it denies any good among the views
of the ancients. This is manifestly untenable. The second
rests on a most peculiar interpretation of the passage in Genesis and cannot be defended. The third is more plausible, but
cannot be proved. In fact there is no evidence whatever that
Plato or any of the great writers of the fifth century had read
Moses. The mere fact that some of them travelled in Egypt
carries no weight. For one must remember two things. First
of all, these Greeks had a strong superiority complex over
against the barbarians. It was not their nature to think that
they could learn anything really worth while from them. But
secondly, the Greeks had no inclination toward learning the
language of those barbarians. How then could they ever have
gotten their ideas from Moses and the prophets?

The view which is most nearly correct is that which explains the phenomena by the presence of Logos. I say this
is most nearly correct. For even here there is a serious omission. In these Apologists scant reference is made to the work
of the Holy Spirit. In fact the Logos work is largely that
which should be attributed to the Spirit of God. The truth
which these apologists bring out by this doctrine of the Logos
is that all is not total darkness outside the realm of Christianity. There are grains of truth. There are rays of light which
presage the great light that arose in Jesus Christ.

It has been stated that this view is most nearly correct. A
more complete statement would be as follows. There is in
Reformed Theology a rather careful distinction about the
revelation of God. It maintains that God has and does reveal

himself in two ways. There is what is called general revelation and again there is special revelation. Even in the world
God does not leave himself without witness. He speaks to
men in pagan nations through their noblest souls and greatest
geniuses. Through them He reveals bits of knowledge about
Himself, the world, and man. He inspires them with high
conceptions about Himself, with exalted ideals for the life of
man. He awakens in them the sense of justice and goodness,
and gives them insight into the folly of the ways of man. He
creates in men respect for law and government, that life in
society and in the state may be possible. Through the history
of a nation and of the race He reveals many beautiful truths
to men utterly unacquainted with Scripture. Such a general
revelation is the cause of the high civilization attained in antiquity. Therein lies the explanation of the glory that was
Greece, and the grandeur that was Rome, to mention only
those two. According to this view all the fine achievements
of the men who live outside the Kingdom of God are the direct result of the revelatory act of God.

But that light is insufficient. Insufficient to give the light
necessary to salvation not only, but also for living in accord
with the will of God. That his nature and will may be known
He himself must speak directly. This He does through the
consciousness on the part of the prophets of old: Thus saith
the Lord. It means a much more direct, more complete revelation than that which is given in and through the mind
and conscience of natural man. It rests on the general revelation, but completes and corrects it and thus makes the revelation final. Scripture is the word of God himself.

The connecting link between the two revelations is the
Christ, the Logos of God. He is the substance, the content
of the revelation, but the Holy Spirit is the means. Therefore
in the Christ we have the full, complete, perfect revelation of
God. He is not only man, speaking because God has laid
hold on him, but He himself is God. And special revelation
centers in the Christ.

All this can be put in another way. Reformed theology also says that there is common and special grace. In common grace and its blessings all men as men can share. Special grace is that which is received by the elect alone. Now, it is the common grace of God which has been given bounteously to the peoples of ancient Greece and Rome. Because of that grace their civilizations attained the heights. Through that common grace Socrates, Plato, Sophocles, Pheidias, Homer, etc., received the insight, into truth and put it in the forms which have come down to us. Side by side with the doctrine of total depravity, the Reformed theologians have put the doctrine of common grace. It is by means of this doctrine that the explanation is found for all the good present in the teaching and the life of people who have never heard the Gospel. A fuller discussion of this doctrine will come in the next chapter.

In the characterization of the doctrine of Common Grace given above and in the next chapter the view as historically held especially by the churches of the Netherlands is presented. That doctrine has been attacked in the United States by the Reverends Herman Hoeksema of Grand Rapids, Mich., and Henry Danhof of Kalamazoo, Mich., but was reaffirmed by the Christian Reformed Church. The controversy led to the deposition of the two ministers and the departure of a large part of their congregations from the ecclesiastical fold of the Christian Reformed Church.

More recently there has been great agitation about the doctrine in the Netherlands. Professor K. Schilder of the Seminary at Kampen was the leading figure among those raising questions relative to the doctrine. The matter called for Synodical action, scheduled for 1939, but the war and later the invasion by Germany temporarily, at least, brought other issues to the fore. Though the position of Dr. Schilder is not entirely clear and consistent, it does seem that he wishes to emphasize the responsibility of the recipient of common grace, and maintains that only the "receiving" has been brought out in the past. He stresses the idea of "duty" because of, rather than that of "gift" thru the grace received. But the views of Schilder on this and other doctrines has led to a schism in the churches of little Holland.

CHAPTER III

Christianity and Paganism

B. *The Modern Views*

THE ANSWER given today may be described as threefold. First there are those who maintain that the doctrines of Christianity are not only unique but quite opposed to all that was found in antiquity. The picture one is asked to call to mind is this. The world of paganism was in a fearful state at the time of the birth of Christianity. Everything was in a state of extreme degradation and deterioration. The world was on a toboggan and was sliding into a state of complete collapse. Things had been getting steadily worse. The views maintained were entirely opposed to what Christianity taught. Morally, religiously, politically, socially, economically, intellectually the world was down and out. There was a state of quite universal bankruptcy. There was no hope in any of the ideas and ideals. Whatever was thought and practiced was quite thoroughly bad.[1]

The up shot of this view is that the world of ancient paganism made no positive preparation for Christianity. It was, in fact, quite contrary to it. The doctrines of Christianity came from another world, and were on all points in conflict with this one. There is no connection between the two. The one is natural and the other is supernatural, and there is no common ground.

The good in this view is the intense desire to uphold the transcendental element in the Christian religion. By all means it exalts the supernatural character of the revelation in Jesus

---

1. Cf. Angus, S: Environment of Early Christianity p. 2.

Christ and thru the apostles. It is zealous to maintain the uniqueness of the religion of Christ. To exalt the supernatural, it loses sight of the natural, or thoroughly degrades it. In its emphasis on the supernatural it strives to hold fast to one of the distinctive features of the Christian religion. But, as the apologists of old, it seems to think that the only way to exalt Christianity is to debase the religious and moral teaching of antiquity. It, however, ignores the fact that God rules the world and that all things serve a purpose determined on by Him.

It seems to favor the idea that in the world outside of Christianity there was no other purpose operating than to display the folly, the weakness, the sin of man. Hence the emphasis on the weaknesses of the age, the descriptions of degradation, selfishness, licentiousness, irreligion, the intellectual decadence, as portrayed in the Roman satirists, historians, and in Paul. However, in the sequel it will be shown that common grace does more than act as a brake to the downward trend of this civilization. The criticism to be levelled at this view is that it is too restrictive with reference to the rule of God, that in consequence it leaves too much of life to be controlled completely by the evil one.

This view described above is held by few people today. The prevalent and popular view at this time is quite the opposite. Under the influence of the philosophical[2] and biological doctrine of evolution the idea has spread widely that all of life is to be accounted for in the same way. The gist of the application of the doctrine to the field of religion is that Christianity also is to be explained in this way. Through a process of generations these doctrines of Christianity had been formulated and at a given time they were combined into what is the teaching of Christianity. The process of development has ultimately culminated in these noble views. It is regarded as a purely natural phenomenon and the "new religion added absolutely nothing new on the subject (theology) to the teach-

---

2. Cf. Case, S. J.: Evolution of Early Christianity pp. 10-11.

ing we still find in Plato or Cicero."[3]   Due to the social, political, moral, religious conditions and beliefs this new religion
slowly took form.   Hence a careful analysis of all the factors
of the environment in the first century will reveal how the
thing came about.   It is all quite natural, due to the interplay
of the forces of life itself.[4]

The weakness in this presentation of Christianity is that
it completely minimizes the element which the former view
so highly exalted.   The first view glorified the supernatural;
this view does the same with the natural.   Accordingly the
religious beliefs and practices in the mystery religions will
explain the origin of much that is cardinal to Christianity.
There is nothing new in the doctrine of the Virgin birth, in
the belief in a Savior-God, in the rites of baptism and communion, in the ethical teaching of the New Testament writings.
It was all present in the pagan world.

The third view is that which characterizes itself as holding
to the good in each of the preceding and yet keeping them in
the balance.   The Reformed view pictures the world of antiquity as neither totally corrupt nor altogether good.   It does
not view the course of the history of the pagan peoples as
only downward on the steep road to the abyss.   Nor again
does it see humanity in antiquity climbing higher and higher
until it finally scales the heights of thought characteristic of
Christian teaching.   Rather it views the situation as a combination of both.   There are trends and movements pointing
upward.   Again there is much that points downwards toward
ruin and destruction.   The Providence of God does not lead
only to a long list of zeros so that the total effect is negative.
But through the negation at times and again along side it in
another direction there is a positive working.   How this
works out in detail will be pointed out later.   It is only neces-

---

3. Farrer, J. A.: Paganism and Christianity p. 30.
4. Cf. Case, S. J.: Evolution of Early Christianity; Carus, P.: Pleroma;
Whittaker, T.: The Origins of Christianity.

sary here to state the view as held by Reformed thinkers over a long period of time.

Before proceeding to a further elucidation we must pause to examine why the Reformed give the explanation as described briefly above. There it was indicated that one view stressed only the supernatural element in Christian thought; the other only a natural. The true view accepts both. Why? Because on the basis of the evidence there is no alternative in Scripture. Let us begin with Jesus. Has not the church confessed of Him through out the ages that he is real man and very God? John said that the Word was with God and was God and became flesh and tabernacled among us[5] Paul states that in the fulness of time God sent forth his son, born of a woman, born under the law[6] In these passages we have the teaching of the nature of the Christ epitomized. He is not only God, nor only man, but both.

If that is the teaching of Scripture the result must be quite obvious. To maintain the true humanity of Jesus one cannot emphasize only the supernatural element, the divinity in him. If real man then environment, the historical conditions must have a real significance also. In eliminating these one goes astray by denying in fact the humanity of Jesus. But just as certainly the other view goes astray. If he is very God, then too it follows that there is in him something which goes above the world of history. There is an element in him which cannot be accounted for by his environment and the course of history which had been run before. Because He is God, there is in Him the supernatural which the world cannot produce.

And likewise in the case of Paul we must emphasize the natural and the supernatural. It is extreme folly to see in him only the working of the natural man. Nor can one read him without feeling that he is conscious of a higher something than himself. He is in the Christ through faith and love, and that Christ is the one who has risen from the dead and as-

---

5. John 1.
6. Gal. 4:4.

cended to the highest heavens. The Spirit of that Christ controls Paul so that he reveals the supernatural. But again it is hazardous to over-emphasize the supernatural in him. His environment and natural soul make-up will not explain Paul, nor on the other hand must they be left out of consideration. The city of Tarsus in which he spent his boyhood was real to him and left its mark. A great meeting place of East and West, home of many of the Stoics, a center of many of the oriental mystery religions, must have influenced Paul, determined something of his thinking and colored his vocabulary. Paul had a normal boyhood and therefore his life is not without contact with historical conditions.

The Reformed view here, as in many other cases, is broader and richer than the others. In this particular case it sees some, yes, much good in pagan thought, but at the same time it maintains the essential difference between it and the teaching of Scripture.[7] This can be done because of the acceptance of a general and special revelation, or again because of its belief in special and common grace. It is the common grace of God which has led the noble souls of antiquity to see and to propagate the excellent ideas and ideals. It is God's grace applied through the operation of the Spirit which explains whatever was good and true in pagan antiquity. The Reformed view denies to the natural man the ability and inclination to discover the perfect truth. Both are due to the general revelation of the Spirit.

Here then we see the difference between the view of the apologists and that of the Reformed thinkers. The apologists at times explained the good as due to the Logos. One objection to that is, as was said there, that the work is really that of the Holy Spirit. But furthermore, that view of the apologists postulated that the Logos was in every man, resident in him. That view approaches dangerously to the Greek. The Reformed view does not make it immanent in man, but explains it as working of the Spirit.

---

7. Bavinck, H.: Calvin and the Reformation, pp. 103-104.

To return now to a further elucidation of this doctrine of common grace as applied to pagan civilization. In surveying that civilization one can maintain that this grace operated not only negatively but also positively.[8] Its sole function was not to restrain the various evil tendencies, to hold sin in check. There was not only a working of the Spirit by which the minds of men saw the inconsistencies and the folly of their views, so that by their reasoning they felt themselves led astray and into deeper struggles. Nor was the only effect such that in their hearts they felt nothing but a vain groping which led to more intense despair. But often through their thinking they came upon bits of truth which gave them a measure of satisfaction and a measure of contentment and joy. It was not all disillusionment in the minds of men.

It was said above that through the negative working, the result at times was positive, or that along side the negative there was another positive current. It is necessary to explain this a little further and a few examples will therefore be given. There is no doubt that the ancient religions of the Greeks and Romans were in a sad plight during the last century before Christ and the first century of the Christian era. Scepticism, doubt, unbelief, mockery, were rife. The Gods had failed them in their critical periods and men as a result forsook them. Criticism of polytheism was met on every hand. But if one now draws the conclusion that therefore the period is one in which irreligion stalks through the lands he is sadly mistaken. For just the contrary was the case. And this criticism of the polytheistic system and the general distrust of the traditional gods and goddesses led to two things. First the criticism of polytheism led men more and more in the direction of a monotheistic conception as is evident in Stoicism. Most thinking people felt that behind all these gods there was one supreme power, that the gods were only individual manifestations of that which lay behind them all. A gradual breakdown of polytheism was accompanied by a ten-

8. Wielenga, G.: Paulus p. 20.

dency toward monotheism, and at the same time to a more noble conception of the gods. Thus along side the negative activity there is also a positive. Through the very breaking down of the old, a new structure, higher and more true, is being built.

Again attention should be directed toward a second most interesting fact which is evidence of the same negative-positive working of the Spirit. Since man is fundamentally religious, the collapse of faith in his old divinities was bound to be accompanied by the creation or importation of new ones. And this last is exactly what happened. The gods of the Graeco-Roman world had failed them in their individual and political life, and therefore the ancient pagans turned their eyes elsewhere. There is remarkable interest in things from the East. Men turned to the older civilizations of Egypt and Asia Minor to look for the gods who served men there. Hence there is a great importation into the Graeco-Roman world of Isis and Osiris, of Cybele, of Demeter, of Mithra. Through the consciousness of failure of their own, there comes a great revival of interest in religions from the East. Thus again the breaking up of their own system is a negative something, but the turning to the East, in the expectation of receiving help from the gods there, is positive.

Take too the example from the intellectual life. When one follows the course of thought from the fifth century B. C. down to the first A. D. there is evident the change from youthful enthusiasm and idealism to disillusionment and scepticism. Originally the Greeks were filled with high hopes; gradually the hopes turned out to be disappointing. One after another of the high ideals failed to give satisfaction. As a result men began to distrust their systems of thought not only, but their ability to find solutions at all. Scepticism increasingly raises its head, and more and more there is a distrust of reason. Men are ready to accept authority, and readily bow before it. There is too a wave of mysticism sweeping over the Mediterranean world. Hence the great popularity of the mystery religions as compared with what had been. Here again there is that same negative-positive action of the Spirit on the souls of men. Through the breaking down of the confidence in reason, came the postive element of finding the road to peace and happiness through the channels of the will and the emotions.

One more example will suffice. In the realm of social life we notice an increased development of individualism. This was but natural. As the Roman eagle spread its wings wider more and more peoples and communities lost their independence. The ancients felt a strong alliance with their native city. When that city then was swallowed up into the colossus of Rome, the individual contact with the city was broken and the individual was thrown back on himself. With the loss of independence of the individual states there was at the same time a development of individualism in the souls of men. Such a development was positively in the direction of Christianity which called for faith on the part of the individual in Jesus Christ and God.

These instances which could be multiplied many times indicates what is meant when it is said that common grace works both negatively and positively. When the various elements of the Graeco-Roman life are discussed later, further evidence will be given of the same thing. Before we turn to those particulars we shall give a description of the civilization of the world into which Christianity came.

CHAPTER IV

The World of the New Testament

To Give an adequate description of the Graeco-Roman civilization in one brief chapter is beyond the realm of the possible. All that can be done is to indicate some of the chief characteristics of that world. To trace the features in detail would be a task requiring volumes. To avoid an account which would be too sketchy the attempt will be made to seize upon the more important, more outstanding characteristics rather than give a complete enumeration.

We in America are accustomed to hearing our nation described as the "melting pot." Into it the blood of all nations has been poured and the peoples of all lands rub shoulders together. Into this one American civilization the tiny streams from all the nations of the earth have emptied themselves.

Something similar happened long ago in the days of what is called the Graeco-Roman, or Hellenistic civilization. That too was a time of the mingling of the peoples of the Mediterranean basin with one another. The Mediterranean world was a seething cauldron in which every type of human idea, every striving, every ambition was found.

The picture is that of one civilization entering as a stream into the river of another nation. Or again one can attempt to describe it as the putting of one layer on another. Always, of course, with the understanding that the relation was not really one of layers. For there was a penetration of the one into the other, the influence of the one on the other. The picture of the streams is more accurate although that suggests too much the total loss of identity. And just that too did not happen. There was a mingling of all peoples, there were contacts but the result was not a loss of identity of the particular nation. Both figures therefore give only a suggestion of what happened during the Hellenistic Age.

There were in the world at that time three outstanding nations who dwelt along the shores of the Mediterranean. At least they were outstanding from the point of view of their influence upon the course of history in Western Europe. These three peoples are the Jews, the Greeks and the Romans. The remarkable thing is that the influence of each of these is traceable to the limits of each of the other two. Or rather, these civilizations lived side by side, each acquainted with and influenced by both of the others. Our purpose is to seek to get at the genius of each people, its major characteristics and achievements, to evaluate that, and to point out its significance in relation to the Advent. Too frequently the idea of the fullness of time has been restricted to external and physical conditions. The preparation for and the contributions to the Advent are then limited to the universal language of the Greeks, the Pax Romana and the good roads and safe travel on land and sea of the Romans. These are very significant elements, but the whole realm of the spirit of the peoples and that in relation to Christianity is passed by. Yet that is surely the more important phase since Christianity is first of all a thing of the spirit. It need hardly be said that just as that is the more significant, it is too immeasurably more difficult. It is no easy task to get at and describe the genius of one's own people. Here we have more than one, existing centuries ago, and in addition to the description we are compelled to give an evaluation. For God did send his Son in the fullness of time.

Let us begin with Israel. From Moses on a long line of seers and singers had spoken to the people of Israel in the name of Jehovah. They were conscious that their words were not their own, but rather were given them from the God of their people. Building on Moses and adding thereto in the process of unfolding the truth of God, prophet after prophet had brought his message. But, as already said, not his own, but the Word of God. This long row of prophets ends with Malachi. We can say that in the Providence of God the revelation of the Old Testament had been completed.

Let us pause for a few minutes to reflect on that history a little further. When one considers what has been said above about general and special revelation and then turns to the history of Israel certain impressions are outstanding. There is in that people, as revealed in the Old Testament, something unique. The contrast between the other two, Greece and Rome is well-defined.[1] The life of this nation expresses itself on a different level; its ideals are of a different character.

According to the Old Testament, Israel is the chosen people. They are favored by Jehovah above all the nations of the earth. And according to a New Testament writer, the oracles of God were entrusted to them. Surely there was a distinctiveness about them. They had something which other nations did not have. That which they had can be described as the fruit of special revelation, or again of special grace.

Since it is not clear to all just what this implies, it is well to look more closely at that history or civilization of Israel. As was said, the perfectly evident thing is that it moves on a higher level. To understand that level, it is necessary to have something of a philosophy of history with reference to Israel. Needless to say, that very philosophy must be built on the data of the Old and New Testaments. In the light of those data, Israel has a peculiar mission. She has a unique task, a very special calling. To them are entrusted the oracles of God.

The true knowledge of God had been lost through the fall of man. Through that fall man's mind was so darkened that he could no longer attain to a correct conception of God and man and the world through his own efforts. All the reflection and meditation, no matter how sincerely intended,

---

1. Cf. Livingstone, R. W.: The Greek Genius and its Meaning to Us, p. 138; Butcher, S. H.: Originality of Greece p. 42.

no matter how zealously carried on, would not bring to man the truth about God, himself and the world. To accomplish that, God Himself must step in. He Himself must reveal Himself, that the world may learn to know Him. The vessel chosen for that high honor is Israel. Unto them God chooses to reveal Himself, and that as to no other nation in the world. Therefore Moses and the prophets and the psalmists speak as they do. This we call the special revelation of God. The mission of Israel lies in the field of special grace.

The peculiar content of that revelation is often briefly described as ethical monotheism. Naturally time cannot be taken to investigate the meaning of this term as it has been applied to the history of Israel from the evolutionary point of view. We must content ourselves with a mere statement of what the term signifies in the light of Israel's history. The essence of the matter is that to Israel is revealed the true conception of one supreme, sovereign God, and that to him are ascribed the highest ethical attributes. To Moses it was revealed that the God of Israel was the only God, and holiness, righteousness, truth, mercy, characterized him. And because God was so conceived and known by the Israelites, a life corresponding to these high conceptions was incumbent on men. God was absolutely righteous and true; hence his people must practice these very things. Be ye holy as I am holy.

It is quite generally agreed that there is this element of distinctiveness in the teaching of the Old Testament.[2] Certainly it is entirely true, if one makes a comparison only between Israel, and Greece and Rome. The task of Israel then, was to receive this revelation from God, and then to make it known unto the world. Because it was such a unique thing, every precaution must be taken to keep it intact. Therefore Israel must be separate from the nations. God's providence leads them to Palestine, away from direct contact with great pagan nations. There the truth is to be gradually unfolded. To preserve it, contacts with pagan nations are to

2. Berdyaev, N.: The Meaning of History, p. 88.

be avoided as much as possible. For association with the pagans will cause a contamination of the pure truth revealed by God about Himself. The Old Testament is replete with instances of that back-sliding due to the fact that Israel is all too eager to look over its national wall.

It was said that this course of revelation goes on until the time of Malachi. This was about 450 B. C. He is the last of the prophets of the Old Testament. The heights of revelation through mere men have now been scaled. If anything additional is to be given, the means to be employed must be of another character. And that is precisely what the New Testament teaches. Formerly God spoke through men in divers ways, but now at the last he speaks through his own Son. The additional revelation must come through the incarnation.

But before that momentous event something else must happen. After Malachi Israel no longer lives in isolation. Rather the nation becomes scattered everywhere throughout the Mediterranean basin. There are many more Israelites among the gentile nations than in Palestine itself. This scattering had been going on since the days of Jeremiah, but increased remarkably in the age after Alexander the Great. In following the travels of St. Paul we see that the sons of Israel are in every city in the Mediterranean world. Over a million live in Alexandria in Egypt. There is a whole colony of them over the Tiber in Rome. In every city Paul goes to a synagogue of the Jews. Hence, long before Paul, the Sibylline oracle of about 140 B. C. says of the Jewish people that "every land and sea was filled with them."[3]

Thus these Jews are as seed sown among all the peoples of the ancient world. Wherever they go they carry with them their high conception of God, and the calling of man to live a morally clean life. The pagan world heard from the lips of these Jews and saw in their lives higher conceptions of the nature and will of God than any found among their own noble

---

3. Orac. Sibyll. III, 271.

thinkers. But if the argument is put forth that these Jews lived their lives in separation and hence the influence of them was not great the fact is lost sight of that the Jew was filled with a proselytizing zeal. The prophets had not proclaimed in vain that Israel was the chosen people and therefore had the high calling to make known unto the nations the message from Jehovah.

But another fact is this. Between the years 250 and 150 B. C. something truly momentous had been done. As these Jews lived one, two, three generations among the pagans, they discovered that their children could no longer read the writings of Moses and the prophets in their own tongue. The language of the academic and mercantile world was Greek. In this time it comes about that the Old Testament is translated into the Greek language and is called the Septuagint. Now the sons of Israel could again read the sacred writings. But that is not all. Now too for the first time the pagans could get a first hand knowledge of these very writings. Thus through the Dispersion and through the Septuagint the Israelite ideas of God and man were spread widely through the ancient world.

When we turn to Greece to view the general trend and history of her civilization we face a totally different kind of people. The Israelites are Orientals but the Greeks are Occidentals. That explains much in the outlook of each. But especially important is the fact that the particular achievement of Israel lay in the field of special grace. This fact has been stated by Bavinck in these words: "Israel was the people of the sabbath, the pagans are the people of the week. In art, science, political science, in all that belongs to the realm of culture, Israel stood far behind many heathen peoples."[4] The achievement of Greece lay in the field of common grace. Of course Israel too enjoyed the fruits of common grace. Life in an organized society is not possible without it. But

4. Bavinck, H.: Het Ryk Gods het Hoogste Goed. In Kennis en Leven p. 30.

the point here is that what was distinctive of each was the result of common grace in the one, and of special grace in the other. And the essential contribution of Israel lay in the field of religion and morality. It is rightly said: "But in religion, and in those matters of personal morality which are apt to be most affected by the state of religious feeling and belief, the Greeks of Aristotle's time were mere children compared with the Jews."[5] The simple fact is that so far as Israel outstripped other nations in its lofty conceptions of God and morality, in like manner she lagged behind in other fields. Hence we do not turn to Israel to find learned discussions on philosophy and science.

That statement may seem strange. By it is meant that we do not find works comparable to those of Plato and Aristotle among the Greeks. To be sure, these Israelites had given the general data for such philosophy and ethics. But the fact is that the mind of the Israelite did not concern itself with a rational, unified, systematized outlook upon life. He believed with all his heart on Jehovah and his will, but did not formulate his beliefs into a system as did the Greeks. His was more the direct, practical, intuitive approach rather than the intellectual. This characteristic of the Hebrew has been described as follows: "The Hebrew mind is intuitive, imaginative, almost incapable of analysis or of systematic connection of ideas. It does not hold its object clearly and steadily before it, or endeavor exactly to measure it; rather it may be said to give itself up to the influence of that which it contemplates, to identify itself with it and to become possessed by it. Its perceptions of truth came to it in a series of vivid flashes of insight, which it is unable to coordinate. For the most part it expresses its thought symbolically, and it constantly confuses the symbol with the thing signified. The Greek mind, on the other hand is essentially discursive, analytical, and systematic, governing itself even in its highest flight

5. Rashdall, H: Conscience and Christ p. 80.

by the idea of measure and symmetry, of logical sequence and connection."[6]

One can describe in a word the difference between the Greek and the Jewish mind by saying that the former is hypotactic and the latter is paratactic. That is to say that the Greek organizes the material logically, arranging it according to its importance and the interrelations of cause, effect, time etc. B and C are related in some way to A. But the Hebrew mind arranges them next to each other, and not even necessarily so that A is first and B second. Read Genesis 1 as a good example. All the items in the account of creation are arranged, apparently coordinately, and connected with "and." Read also the Book of Proverbs or Ecclesiastes. One verse says, "Answer the fool according to his folly," the other says "Answer the fool not according to his folly." Now the Greek would attempt to say when you should do the one, and when the other. But of all that there is nothing in the Hebrew mind. So too in Ecclesiastes, "There is a time for weeping and a time for laughing." In the field of mathematics the relation of the circumference of the circle to its diameter was apparently unknown. cf. I Kings 7:23 and II Chronicles 4:2. In none of the fields of natural science, political science, the arts of literature, sculpture, and painting did Israel have the preeminence. And all these are the gifts of common grace. They are not the element which make up the vital relationship between God and man.

When men speak of the glory that was Greece they have exactly these things in mind. It is therein that Greece rose to unprecedented heights. Never before in the history of the world had such masterpieces been produced. All those at home in the fields of architecture and sculpture pay tribute to Greece which becomes the source of emulation and envy. Men may, they say, equal what the Greeks have done but they cannot surpass them. Further, the highest excellence was

---

6. Caird, E.: Evolution of Theology in Greek Philosophy Vol. II, pp. 188-189.

attained in many literary forms.   Epic, dramatic, lyric poetry,
historical, philosophical, oratorical prose all cast in superla-
tive form are the achievement of Greece.   These productions
in the realm of the beautiful have served as the inspiration
and model for the work of the generations down to the present.

This genius of the Greek people is characterized by supreme
achievements in three directions.   There was with them an
intense love of knowledge, of the beautiful, and of freedom.
The rather remarkable fact is first that they had a soul expressing itself in all these ways, but more than that, that
the achievement in each direction was paramount.   If one
knows something of the history of civilization it becomes
clearer what an amazing achievement this was.   It is then
comparatively easy to find a nation surpassing others in one
direction.   It is quite another thing to find a nation so gifted
that it attains the preeminence in a number of fields.

For these three loves, love of knowledge, of beauty, of freedom are all too frequently found to exist separately.   This
applies to both the individual and the nation.   Love of knowledge strikes the intellectual note, love of beauty the aesthetic
and emotional, love of freedom the volitional.   The remarkable thing is that the Greeks had all three and in a rather full
measure.

A brief glance at the course of western civilization will
make this more evident.   The Greeks reached the very heights
in the directions of the intellect and the feeling, in the sense
of the aesthetic.   Their weakest link was that of action.   Even
here it must not be supposed that they lagged far behind.
For their continued effort at the attainment of freedom, even
at great odds, stands out as a shining example.   They were
willing not only to talk about freedom, but even to fight and
die for it.   They did achieve, as well as think and feel.   The
contrast with the Romans is very glaring.   However much
one may extol the Romans for their mighty works, he cannot rightly credit them with any outstanding intellectual and
aesthetic capabilities.   Therein they themselves recognized

the Greeks, largely took over from them, and then adapted and used for their own purposes. As one passes on he finds intellectual activity almost eclipsed in the dark ages, as well as that of the feeling in the higher sense. Slowly the mind of men again began to be active, really so in scholasticism. But both the aesthetic and the volitional are highly defective. And as the intellect steadily rises in the Renaissance together with the aesthetic, the moral plummets downward. Moving on to our contemporary America one can hardly maintain with justice that the intellectual part of man is rising to higher levels, altho there is an increased emphasis on the aesthetic.

Because of the significance for their own outlook upon life, and the influence this trait of love of knowlege had on the early church, a more detailed account of the specific content of the term will be enlightening. This is the more true since Western civilization since the Renaissance has often glorified it as the outstanding characteristic of the Greeks.

This love of knowledge was first of all a true inquisitiveness. The world of phenomena, of facts, in which he lived was not merely accepted. The Greek had a mind which was alert to itself and to its environment and therefore was curious about the phenomena. Reflection, thought, analysis, understanding of the universe were native to him. He had an intense desire simply to know. The contrast between Greek and Oriental, especially Babylon and Egypt, is marked. The Egyptians, like the Romans later, had a rudimentary knowledge of geometry. Their chief concern, however, was to be able to use it after the inundations of the Nile. Hence the knowledge remained rudimentary, and was not systematized. But the Greeks went far beyond that. Already in the days of Plato (427-347 B. C.) students were led into higher mathematics. The Greek wanted to know simply for the sake of knowing. His course, though not unrelated to the practical, was not determined by the practical. This is evident too from his interest in the heavenly bodies. Egyptians and Baby-

Ionians were interested from a practical angle. They could then determine the course of events in the life of the individual. Hence we have astrology among them. The Greek looked much further and was interested in knowing the movement of the heavenly bodies for its own sake.

Again this love of knowledge was characterized by its having no limits. The point is not that Greek knowledge was complete. He himself realized only too well that in many cases it was extremely fragmentary. But his desire to know had no limitation as to the objects of which he might gain knowledge. Here again he differed from the Oriental who was more mystical and had a greater sense of awe. The Oriental therefore had a feeling that there were territories not to be explored; there were boundaries beyond which man should not go. There were taboos in the realm of the intellect. The mind must not seek to know beyond definite limits. Over against that the Greek knew no restrictions. Nothing was secret in the sense that one might not attempt to know it. With his clear intelligence he felt privileged to inquire into all things, both human and divine. The world and the fullness thereof was his field of operation. This is evident from the fact that there were investigators of every department of learning.

A third characteristic is the Greek desire to know beyond mere form and appearance. There are explicit statements, as well as the general trend, to prove that the Greek wanted to know the underlying cause of things. He was not satisfied with numerous data, but wished an understanding and analysis of the data. Thus early Greek philosophy sought diligently for the ultimate substance which lay beyond the particulars. A few examples will make this clear. This explains Thucydides' careful account of the causes of the ruinous Peloponnesian War between Athens and Sparta. It explains too his eager desire to know why the fearful plague fell on Athens. It gives insight into Aristotle's careful discrimination of the four kinds of causes. It explains too the working of the majestic minds of Aeschylus and Sophocles in dramatizing the lot of mortals in tragic fashion.

Summarizing this love of knowledge we can say that it expressed itself in the desire to define, to speculate, and to systematize. Just because the Greek did not merely accept the universe, he asked himself what the thing really was. He was not satisfied merely to know that something existed. He wanted to know what it was, and therefore had to define, delimit it, as over against other things. One of the best examples of this tendency is to be found in the dialogues of Plato. Socrates asked, what is temperance, or moderation, what is holiness, what is friendship, what is justice? And because the Greek set no limits to his inquiry he speculated far beyond the mere phenomena. He knew no limits. Hence he courageously followed the argument whithersoever it led. He was not restrained by the fear that he might go too far, or into territory upon which there was to be no trespassing. Because he was interested in causes and the cause he dared to speculate about that which would explain satisfactorily the particulars. And withal he sought unity, system. Because he took into consideration all things and because he wanted to understand each particular he was driven to systematization. He wanted a totality view in which everything, clearly apprehended and defined, had its own place.

This element of the Greek spirit had great influence on, and made definite contributions to the Christian movement in the first three centuries. At the same time it was the factor which was operative at the bottom of some of the heresies which arose. It was the tendency to define, to speculate, to systematize that put the givens of the revealed Word into creeds. From that Greek spirit comes the formulation of the belief in the Trinity with its interpretation of the relation of the Son to the Father, and of the Holy Spirit to both. It was this Greek spirit that defined and delimited the nature and work of the Logos. It made of Christian teaching a system, a unity, in which all the givens of Scripture are taken up. The history of dogma shows that all these questions of ultimate reality are faced and answered by the Eastern or Greek church. The Roman spirit concerned itself with more practical matters of the Christian faith. This love of knowledge is ultimately the explanation of Gnosticism in the church. It had, at times, led to wild, fantastic, and wholly unwarranted speculations, which led far from the truth of Scripture.

The second great love of the Greeks was of the beautiful. We shall, however, devote less space to it than to the first. That is not because it is less important or less characteristic of the Greek. In fact a good case could be made for its being the foremost characteristic. It is, however, less important for our particular study. To be sure this love of the beautiful does enter into the church, but not noticeably in the first three centuries. As an influencing factor on the early church it is less significant. As an element in their view of life it was extremely important.

We shall therefore make only a few general remarks. The first is that beauty occupied a really important place in their lives. To many in our industrial civilization, beauty is an adjunct, an appendix. It is not, or at least was not regarded as vitally necessary. It is there to be appreciated and practiced by a few. The rest regard it as a fine accomplishment, but it plays no important part in their lives. On that score the ancient Greek was altogether different. Beauty was not merely a luxury in life; it constituted a real necessity. The Greek felt that something essential to life was lacking if beauty was absent. Life was incomplete without it. That explains his interest in athletics for the young and old. He loved to look on beautiful bodies. It accounts for the popularity of costly religious processions. It gives an insight into why his language was fashioned as it was; why his city was adorned with sculptures, memorials, beautiful temples.

Because beauty occupied such an important place the Greek was not satisfied to see it only in adornment. Rather the beauty of the Greek is to be seen in the whole. It consisted of harmony, of unity, of symmetry. It was not placed on the outside, but all the lines and curves, in due relation to the whole, made the object beautiful in the eyes of the Greek. That explains the Greek temples; that also accounts for the perfection of the ideal form in sculpture.

When we say that the Greek loves freedom, it is correct to associate with it the idea of political freedom. He hated tyranny; he himself must have a hand in the making of the laws. But freedom meant much more than that. It included freedom of speech, freedom of bodily movement, freedom in the realm of thought, freedom of religion. It contained a strong measure of individualism, of independence, of non-interference.

On the score of freedom there is a marked contrast between Jew and Greek. It is quite evident from the whole of the Old Testament that the Jew was a strong believer in the law which is given to them by God through the agency of Moses. Law was to him something externally promulgated and demanding his adherence and obedience. Now the Greek was not by any means an anarchist. He too believed in law but that of a different kind. His respect for and obedience to it was not in the first place to something external to him, imposing its demands and restrictions from without, but rather an inner, personal, conscious acquiescence. Law must come from within, and that from without was tyranny. The Greek love of freedom meant exactly not to hem him in and build fences around him on the outside. That constituted for him legalism. But the Jew, as we have seen, had no objections to that at all. Need it be pointed out then that western civilization has had both of these strains in its midst ever since? Which must it be? Freedom as determined by the individual himself or as imposed on him from without?

This Greek genius had reached unprecedented heights in the fifth century B. C. and the center of that Greek life was in Athens. There the great sculptors, architects, dramatists, philosophers, poets, produced their masterpieces. In these fifth and fourth centuries democracy was the ideal of the common man. But when the two great sections of the Greek people, Athens and Sparta, had exhausted themselves in war against one another others rose up to gain the mastery. Philip of Macedon comes on the scene, and he is followed by the still greater Alexander, to be called the Great.

Alexander is most significant for our study, because it is he who feels himself called to conquer all other nations and to spread this marvelous Greek civilization throughout the then known world. He goes forth to conquer. Down the eastern shore of the Mediterranean, into Egypt, on to Babylon, and even to India the armies of Alexander go. The purpose is to spread Greek culture among all peoples.

From Greece itself then flows an activity by which Greek civilization is made to penetrate among civilized and barbarian peoples. To the East and to the West the civilization spread. As was the case with the Jews, so again it is with the Greeks. In Spain, in Italy, in Palestine, in Syria, Africa the culture predominant was Greek. That is why the period after Alexander is called the Hellenistic Age. The Hellenes and the Hellenic spirit have penetrated into all the peoples living in the Mediterranean basin. It is Greek learning, Greek art, Greek science that rules the culture of the time. The Roman poet sighs that conquered Greece has subdued her conquerors. For, though Roman arms defeated Greek, the Greek spirit and genius vanquished the Romans. Hence we have the second layer of a peculiar civilization spread through this ancient world.

And now the Romans. Though they too shared in a large measure of common grace, their achievements are radically different from those of Greece. The character of the people was neither strongly intellectual nor artistic, as was that of the Greeks. Their stronghold in the realm of achievement lay in the direction of the practical and the utilitarian. Two quotations will suffice. Cicero says, "With the Greeks geometry was regarded with the utmost respect, and consequently none were held in greater honor than mathematicians, but we Romans have restricted this art to the practical purposes of measuring and reckoning."[7]   In the next century Seneca wrote: "It was once a foible confined to the Greeks to inquire into what number of rowers Ulysses had, whether the Iliad or the Odyssey was written first, whether they belong to the same author, and various other matters of this stamp."[8]   In the field of organization, of institution, of military conquest, of law and the science of government they rose to heights never attained before.   But in the finer things of life the Romans were compelled to accept from others and to imitate. Roman literature had before it the fine models of the Greeks and it made use of them.   Roman sculpture was mostly an imitation of what the Greeks had done.   In depth of thought there is nothing comparable to the great works of originality of Plato or Aristotle.   The philosophies of the Romans are Stoicism, Epicureanism, and a bit of Platonism and Aristotelianism.   But all this is distinctly derived from the Greeks.   The authors themselves acknowledge their dependence.   Nevertheless they had a strong genius for working over the material at hand and expressing it in forceful and lucid language.

The great achievement of the Romans was in the field of military organization and political control.   Their armies went forth to conquer Europe, reaching even to Great Britain, Around the Mediterranean they conquered and controlled all territory from Spain to the Near East.   To facilitate continued control they built excellent roads, and they made the seas safe from pirates.   In a word they gave the world the Pax Romana.

The course of history is no longer from the East to the West.   The Israelites moved especially from the East westward around the Mediterranean.   The Greeks went both west and east so that they also were found everywhere.   So too

7. Cicero: Tusculan Disputations I. 2. 4-5.
8. Seneca: On the Brevity of Life XIII. 2.

the Romans moved in all directions until the then inhabited world, as it was known, was under their control. Thus the third layer of civilization spread through the Mediterranean area.

It will be worthwhile to restate in a few words the situation as it has been described. The result of our investigation is that the civilization of the world of the New Testament is made up of three main strands. Throughout the Roman world at the time of the Advent there were three civilizations mingling and mixing one with the other. The Jew had gone forth or had been taken from his native land and was influencing life everywhere. The Greek with his ideas and ideals was equally ubiquitous. And likewise Roman legions, tax-gatherers, governors and as a result Roman institutions and practices were also found everywhere. The superscription on the cross is conclusive evidence that these three lived side by side. And it is significant that each of these, independently of the other and each in its own field had reached the heights. Israel by about 450 B. C. had received the last word from the inspired prophets. So too Greece had seen its glorious age in the fifth and fourth centuries. Henceforth in the Hellenistic Age their achievements were to be brought to the attention of the world.

Looking at the contribution which each was to make the following can be said. From Israel comes into the world not only the revelation in the Old Testament, but in Jesus Christ and his apostles comes the final truth. He is the Way, the Truth, and the Life. In the main, as touching all the essential and fundamental teachings of Christianity, both as to morals and religion, the source is to be found in Israel. The content comes from Israel. But Greece through its severe thinking had been led to grapple with ultimate problems. Furthermore they had fashioned a language in which the height and depth of thought could be expressed quite adequately. For, to express somewhat adequately the full divine truth a fine instrument had to be forged. And that the Greek language is. But the contribution of the Greeks in this field does not stop with the New Testament documents. When Christianity was called upon to defend itself and therefore to formulate its own beliefs this Greek spirit and language were ready to be used. It was the influence of the Greek spirit which asked the what, the wherefore, the why, the how. To the ultimate questions the Greek spirit could and did give something like an adequate answer and formulation. It is rightly said that "Dogma in its conception and development is a work of the Greek spirit on the soil of the gospel."[9] The contribution of the Romans is to make this content and form possible of propagation. Because the Roman Empire extended so widely, St. Paul could travel with comparative safety and ease whithersoever he felt called to bring the gospel. The mighty force of Rome ruled and gave peace to the world.

The chief contributory forces in the world of the New Testament have been indicated. The total impression which one should have is that of mixture. The East moved west and the West moved east. Not only Israel but other oriental peoples influenced Greece and Rome. The last centuries before Christ are therefore a conglomerate something. The barriers between the nations had been broken down. As a result there is an increased sense of brotherhood among men. Because the city states of Greece and Rome had been swallowed up in the Empire which was distant and abstract, individualism grew by leaps and bounds. At the same time men felt more for their fellows and the attitude toward slaves became more humane.

The life of the Hellenistic Age was a strange mixture. Epicureanism and Stoicism flourished side by side. The one exalted pleasure as the end of living; the other glorified wisdom. Oriental asceticism crept in. All philosophical schools had their adherents. Platonism, Aristotelianism, Empiricism, Scepticism, could all count their followers. Ardent enthusiasm for learning, as well as distrust of all knowledge. Stern

---

9. Harnack, A.: History of Dogma, Vol. 1, p. 17.

morality and licentiousness lived side by side. Seriousness of purpose and honesty of effort were found as well as bland cynicism, indifference, despair. The old mythology, perforated by arguments of philosophers, still held an important place among the populace. To some, devotion to the gods was a serious task, to others a mere formality. Still others denied the existence of these gods. And others relegated them to the high heavens where they lived in supreme indifference to the affairs of men. Noble intellectual conceptions of the gods held sway among some, among others mysticism ran riot. It was an age of magic, of wonder-working. A profound distrust characterized some. Again there was confidence and hope. There was a general hope of a Savior-God who was looked for among the religions of the East. Briefly it was a world in which every idea and ideal could be found, contending the one with the other, and zealous in the effort to win men to its side.

Reflecting on this history one is tempted to ask why this should be. What was the purpose of it all? Surely this vast movement must have a special relation to the Advent. If the world was being prepared for the coming of the Christ, there must be special meaning in this course of events.

In the narrative of the history of Israel and Greece the difference between the two national ideals becomes apparent. Israel excelled in religion and morality. Greece reached the heights in the field of culture. Even though Israel's outlook was not totally "jenseitig" i. e. other-wordly, there was a strong learning toward it. And surely Greece was "diesseitig", of this world. But Christianity comes as the fulfillment of all that went before. It is more inclusive than all the other views of life. It is broader and richer. It holds up the perfect ideal of the full realization of all of man's capacities. It looks not only to time but to eternity as well. As over against mere humanism it places the importance of and duties toward the divine. Everything comes within its sweep.

Now Israel had genuine religion and morality, but fell short in culture. Greece had that. But the ideal of Christian teaching is not the one or the other but both. The fully developed man is not to be only religious but must be able to express himself in and be appreciative of the cultural side of life as well. In order that this full ideal of life might be realized it was necessary that Israel be made acquainted with that which was not its glory. But too, Greece must be brought into contact with that which it so sadly lacked. To accomplish this these nations were all made to mingle with each other in the period of the Hellenistic Age.

Through it all runs a sovereign purpose. The world is about to become acquainted with the perfect ideal of life. Then first through these contacts each nation must learn to see its own deficiency. Here again, we have that same working of grace in the negative and positive way at the same time. Negatively each saw what itself lacked. And positively it admired the good of the other. The ideal of life was about to be declared to be a combination of both. Religion alone is not the complete fulfillment of man's calling. Much less is culture alone. Christianity has room for both religion and culture. It may have a definite view of the value of each, and that too in relation to one another. But it does hold up as the ideal that man should acquire both. Then it will no longer be Jew or Greek, but that which transcends both by taking up into itself the essential part of each. That is what Christianity does.

CHAPTER V

Greek Thought in the New Testament

INTO THAT WORLD as described briefly in the preceding chapter Christianity came. At this stage it is necessary to inquire into the amount of direct evidence for the mingling of the two. How much contact is manifest in the writings themselves? We shall not now discuss the ideas expressed but face the question simply of evidence of direct influence through quotation or reference.

Jesus himself left no writings. His life is recorded in broad sketches in the Synoptic gospels of Matthew, Mark, and Luke. Because he never left his native Palestine the background of the Synoptics is that of Israel. And because he restricted his calling in the flesh to the house of Israel there is no record of his being in contact with the people of other nations. The only possible exception to this statement is the case of the Syro-Phoenecian woman, and it is by no means certain that she was really a Greek. It is highly probable that she merely spoke Greek. There are, to be sure, passages in which Jesus teaching stands out as contrary to that of the gentiles. His ideals are not their ideals. It is not maintained that Jesus had no direct knowledge of the pagan world. Only this is meant. The teaching of Jesus is not given in a pagan setting, because a pagan had come to see him and to ask him a question. He knew a great deal about Rome, its power and ambitions. But the environment, the background of his teaching is not only Palestinian but Jewish.

With the exception of the Prologue the situation in the fourth gospel is identical. Here too we find ourselves on Palestinian soil. The whole background of the gospel narrative

is Israelitish.   There is only one instance which generally is
interpreted differently.[1] In this passage reference is made to
the Greeks who came to see Jesus.   The question is whether
by the "Greeks" are meant those who were Greeks, by birth,
and nationality and culture, or whether they were Jews who
had become Hellenized.   There seems to be little doubt that
these were real Greeks.   At least they were not Jews of the
dispersion who had acquired Greek habits, outlook, and culture.   The term here employed means those who are not Jews.

The incident then concerns real Greeks.   But even at that
the passage has no direct contribution to make, because the
setting is in Palestine, and the Greeks are thrust into the background after their approach.   It is true that in the interpretation of the passage one can discover a most striking teaching
for the Greeks.   For Jesus points out to them not the way
of enjoyment but that of self-sacrifice and suffering, a way
which is contrary to their outlook generally.

In the Prologue we find ourselves in the midst of terminology which was used by the Greeks.   But since there is no
exact reference we shall take the matter up in a succeeding
chapter which will be devoted to the Logos here spoken of.

In passing from the evangelists to Paul we do much more
than go from one author to another.   We at the same time
pass beyond the borders of Palestine.   For this Paul answered
the call of the Macedonian and was busily engaged in pro-
claiming the gospel in the centers of Greek and Roman civilization.   We now find ourselves thrown into the midst of
Greek life, at Athens, Corinth, Philippi, Thessalonica, and
Ephesus.

Even though Paul had remained a worker in the cities and
villages of Palestine, the contact with and influence of the
non-Jewish world would have been more pronounced in his
case.   For he was born at Tarsus, and was a citizen by birth
of the Roman Empire.   The significance of Paul's birth and
early training at Tarsus is not to be underestimated.   Indeed

---

1. John 12:20 ff.

this city was most excellently equipped to bear and rear the Apostle to the Gentiles. Tarsus was unique among the cities of antiquity. More than others it was the meeting place of East and West. In it there was all that which was typically oriental, but also the Hellenic spirit had entered in a marked degree. In that city, which revealed at close range the contrasting civilizations, Paul grew up. The question of the Hellenic element in Paul therefore becomes extremely important. In addition to the externals of Greek civilization, that it was like a Greek city-state governing itself in internal matters and striking its own coinage, Tarsus could boast of having some of the finest attainments of the Hellenic world. For it was known as a center of Greek learning and it had in its midst a university. In fact it was a seat of the Stoic philosophy, rivalled according to Strabo, only by Alexandria. It was here or in neighboring towns that such as Athenodorus, Antipater, Archedemus, Aratus, and Chrysippus taught. With full justification, therefore, could Paul say that he was a citizen of no mean city.

It will ever remain a most difficult task to determine exactly how far this Hellenic environment influenced Paul. The matter cannot be settled finally because the data on his early life are so meager. The result is that there are two widely divergent views, as that of Ramsay who claims for Paul a regular philosophical Greek education, and that of Sabatier who sees in Paul nothing but the Jew, and attributes nothing to his Hellenistic surroundings. Some argue that because of Paul's Jewish heritage and his birth from the lower class of society he was never really touched by the highest products of Greek literature. Others take the opposite extreme that he had read all the great works of the Greeks and was quite saturated with their views. Thus we read, "And though his father had seen to it that the boy should grow up an adept in the lore of the Jewish people, he had not neglected his secular studies, but had also engaged a special teacher of Greek literature. Thus Paul grew up as many Hellenized Jews did in his day, with a thorough knowledge of the books and culture of the surrounding world."[2] And again, "He (Paul) knew it (Sophocles'Oedipus Rex) as he knew many other master-pieces of the theater, from his student days in Tarshish."[3]

Neither position makes a strong appeal. Paul was a He-brew of the Hebrews and that precludes his being influenced too greatly. He never reveals himself in later life as a Philo who was quite enamored of Plato. Fact is that if Paul were so completely acquainted with Greek literature and philoso-phy one would expect more traces of it. The direct evidence is exceedingly meager. For there are only three such passages from Greek literature. The first is the quotation, "For we are also his offspring."[4] This appears first in Aratus and was repeated a little later by Cleanthes. Again Paul quotes a say-ing of the comic poet Menander in the words, "Evil compan-ionships corrupt good morals."[5] Finally in the epistle to Titus we read that, "the Cretans are always liars, evil beasts, idle guttons."[6] This is found in Epimenides.

What then can be legitemately concluded on the basis of this evidence? Especially when we consider the character of the quotations, or shall we rather say sayings. For if we state that these are quotations we have already said too much. There is not the slightest evidence that Paul had read Menan-der and Epimenides. The words quoted from these two poets are clever utterances, almost proverbial in character. And if one remembers how the sayings from Menander were on the lips of everyone in the Hellenistic world, there is not the least necessity for concluding a personal acquaintance with his writings. The one was a wise-saw, and the other a clever jibe at the Cretans. There was ample opportunity for Paul to have heard them repeatedly instead of assuming that the

2. Asch, S.: The Apostle p. 76.
3. idem p. 425.
4. Acts 17:28.
5. I Cor. 15:33.
6. Titus 1:12.

only conclusion is that Paul had read the works of Menander and Epimenides.

The situation is comparable to this. It has become a byword of the English speaking world that "all the world is a stage." Rash, however would be the conclusion that all who use it have really read Shakespeare. In fact many who use the expression may even be unaware of its origin. It has become almost a proverbial utterance and cannot be regarded as the result of personal acquaintance with the works of Shakespeare.

The instance from Aratus or Cleanthes is slightly different. Aratus (fl. 270 B. C.) wrote: "From Zeus let us begin; him do we mortals never leave unnamed; full of Zeus are all the streets and all the market-places of men; full is the sea and the heavens thereof; always we all have need of Zeus. For we are also his offspring."[7] And Cleanthes wrote as follows: "Hail King for thou are able to enforce obedience from all frail mortals because we are all thine offspring, the image and the echo only of thy eternal voice."[8]

If then we remember the Stoic influence in Tarsus in which Paul grew up, there is no good reason for thinking that he had not read the poem of Aratus or Cleanthes. All the writings of Paul testify to a close acquaintance with the philosophy of Stoicism. And this speech on the Areopagus testifies to the same thing.

In fact a careful analysis gives evidence of close similiarity in expression to what we read in Seneca, the Stoic. Acts 17:24 is paralleled by "The whole world is the temple of the immortal gods."[9] When one reads the twenty-fifth verse he can readily think of "God wants not ministers. How so? He himself ministereth to the human race. He is at hand everywhere and to all men."[10] And again verse twenty-seven permits of the same. Seneca says, "God is near thee; He is

---

7. Aratus: Phenomena 1-5.
8. Cleanthes: Hymn to Zeus 1-4.
9. Seneca: De Benef. VII 7.
10. Seneca: Ep. Mor. XCV 47.

with thee; He is within."[11]   Parallel to verse twenty-nine we read: "Thou shalt not form him of silver and gold: a true likeness of God cannot be mouled of this material."[12]

Thus both the view of no acquaintance at all with pagan literature and that of being fully at home in it seem to be extreme. If Paul had read the masters in Greek philosophy and literature would it not be natural to find more direct evidence of such an acquaintance? On the other hand it is not necessary to accept that Paul was a stranger to it all. He was a generally well-educated and cultured man. Furthermore, he had breadth of interest and contact, together with an inquiring and thinking mind. Surely then one would expect that such an individual who travelled up and down through that Mediterranean world would turn to the papyri rolls of the great writers of the Greek world which left its traces on every hand. But that in no way means that the dominant tone in Paul's thinking on religious and moral questions became Greek, or that his mind was filled with their utterances. Fact is that in all the fundamental views on the ultimate questions of God, man, and the world Paul is essentially Hebrew. The scanty references in his writings are conclusive evidence.

But as he grew up in the oriental-Greek city of Tarsus many of the surface elements of that life would naturally fix themselves in his mind and way of expressing itself. Later as an itinerant preacher he again came into a living contact with the views and utterances of that Hellenistic world. As his being reared in a city left its impress on his vocabulary and imagery, so too that Graeco-Roman world would leave its mark. We therefore find metaphors in Paul such as we find in the Stoics. By both life is pictured as a warfare in which the wise man and the saint are contending for victory against the forces of evil. To gain the victory in the battle both draw attention to the parallel arduous preparation of the entrants in the athletic contests. In both the fight is on against the

---

11. Idem XLI, 1.
12. Idem XXXI, 11.

flesh. To sustain the body properly some can endure only milk, while others more hardy and mature can use solid food. And again both Paul and the Stoics regard life as a pilgrimage to another world.

These all are similarities in expression. The question of agreement or difference in meaning will be taken up later. For it is not warranted to conclude that the views are in fundamental agreement just because the words and expressions in a few instances happen to be found in both Paul and the Stoics.

CHAPTER VI

Is There a God?

THE GROUND traversed thus far may be regarded largely as preliminary to the investigation. At the outset it was stated that a careful appraisal of both movements is necessary in order to reach a conclusion. In the following chapters such an investigation and appraisal will be undertaken. As a conquence there will of necessity be some detailed argumentation, but we must try to keep the essential elements in mind. The matters to be investigated lie chiefly in the domains of religion and ethics. With the exception of this and the following three chapters the considerations lie more directly in the field of ethics. The reasons for this are twofold. It was said by Cicero that Socrates brought philosophy down from heaven to earth.[1] The subject of investigation was no longer the ultimate nature of matter, but Socrates turned the eye within and tried to know himself and his fellow man. The speculations about the world generally were not of interest to him. At least not so long as the vital questions about man were still perplexing him and remained unsolved. Whatever the heights which Plato scaled, the simple fact is that the influential schools of philosophy in the Graeco-Roman world were neither the Platonists nor the Aristotelians but the Stoics and the Epicureans. And each of these was a very practical philosophy. One might say that it was a way of life which they taught. To be sure, Stoicism did speculate on ultimates, but the major emphasis is on the life to be lived here and now. Further, one could hardly expect the Romans to be interested in abstract metaphysical questions. The reading of Cicero,

---

1. Cicero: Tus. Disp. V, 4, 10.

if one will call him a philosopher, of Marcus Aurelius, Epitetus, and Seneca will convince anyone of the truth of this statement. The ground of comparison of the two systems of Stoicism and Christianity will therefore be essentially in the field of ethics.

In recent years much emphasis has been placed on the so-called Mystery religions and their relation to primitive Christianity. Some twenty-five years ago there was a wave of enthusiasm for these Mysteries as though here at last the key to the whole problem had been found. The various points of similarity between them and Christianity were pointed out and identity was therefore assumed. But more recently a much soberer and saner view has been taken. Scholars generally no longer hold those views, and recognize that the solution is not nearly so simple as had been supposed. Now the contrasts and the conflicts loom much larger than at that time.

That the Mysteries, in the main importations from Egypt and the East, were active and popular in the Graeco-Roman world is abundantly evident. Why were they so popular? Some of the chief factors were the following. First of all, they made an appeal to the individual, and that without considerations of race, social status, or sex. Then there was the emotional appeal of the mysterious with its pageantry, its peculiar rites promising release, redemption and ecstatic experience to the initiates. And lastly in them was promised an immortality of happiness. All these factors were missing in the official state religion. Especially the first and last agree with the teaching of Christianity. But the latter rested on the solid basis of an historical individual and not on mythological beings. Nor again did it promise blessed immortality through mysterious magical rites, but through a childlike and living faith in the historically resurrected person of the very Son of God. And as to their affect upon primitive Christianity it is well to bear in mind "that though in Egypt and the Asiatic provinces they had long flourished, in the Western

Mediterranean area it was only after Christianity had obtained a firm foothold that the mysteries began to have vogue."[2] This statement is true especially of Mithraism.

The core of genuine religion as revealed in both the Old and the New testaments is God. The God concept determines everything else. Standing on that basis the Calvinistic interpretation of Scripture has always emphasized the sovereignty of God and the glory of God. It then becomes necessary to inquire whether the Graeco-Roman and the Christian teaching on this doctrine are identical or nearly so.

To do so it is not necessary to give a complete summary of all the attributes of God. The outstanding question is as to the personality of God. After one has read a large amount of Greek and Roman literature and then conscientiously compares it with the Old and the New Testaments, it is inescapable to observe that the general tone is entirely different. The simple fact is that in the Scripture one is constantly brought face to face with a personal God. It is exactly that which gives vitality to Scripture.

When one reads the noblest thoughts of the Greeks and Romans he has no such experience. God is not a person but an abstraction. The mind of man reflecting on itself and the world, in its endeavors to understand them comes to conclusions with reference to the universe. In and behind it all there is that which gives it meaning. Behind all the particulars there is that which is not so. Over against that which is ever changing there is that which changes not. In contrast with that which is ever becoming is that which ever was. The world for the Greek was an ordered, systematized something. In a word a cosmos. That which brings order out of chaos, is the working of mind or intelligence. Hence the emphasis on Nous and Logos in Greek thought. It was final or ultimate reason which reflected and expressed itself in the changing phenomena of the world. Call them Platonic ideas, or what

2. Macgregor, G. A, & Purdy, A. C.: Jew and Greek, Tutors to Christ. p. 274.

you will, the essential thing is that Thought, Reason, Mind, Intelligence was the ultimate, the final thing. And that is an abstraction. The distance between that and the concept of a personal God is infinite. God for the Greeks is an abstract, strictly logical deduction, and, as a result an impersonal being.

A brief survey of the history of Greek thought will make the point clearer. The early philosophers, after reflection on the world, concluded that there was an elemental principle which lay in and behind all the particulars. It was called fire, water, air, or the limitless. But never is the element of personality stressed. Thales extolled the unity of this principle. Anaximander added the idea of infinity. Heracleitus sees it as the source of all activity and hence stresses the element of causality. Parmenides glorifies it as the One, and hence views it as unchangeable. However excellent these may be there is in them all that which on the one hand marks them as conclusions and abstractions of the mind, and on the other as lacking the intensely personal element as it reveals itself in the Old Testament.

In the thinkers of Greece who followed the early philosophers the same phenomenon is to be observed. There was in nature something supernatural, something of a divine power. But men did not interpret this in the sense that it was the action of a personal being or beings. Even the Greek word for God (theos) does not suggest a personal God, and they frequently speak of, "the divine" "to theion" in the neuter. In the case of Plato there are those who argue for a personal God, because the essential element of personality, i.e. purposiveness is found.[3] Though the high moral tone and the zeal with which Plato writes in the tenth book of the laws are inspiring, yet Plato's god turns out to be more the absolute Reason and Goodness, rather than a personal being. He or it is far too distant to enter into actual communion with men. And that is exactly the point. Not what we think God to be,

3. Taylor, A. E.: Plato p. 492.

but what men in the stress and struggle of life find God to be. Accordingly the statement by Demos is much nearer the truth: "But in so far as the Christian God is a supernatural being, personal, good, one, it may be argued that he is a being different from Plato's god. Plato's theology is tinged with polytheism; he speaks of gods no less than god, and the references to demons[4] are frequent in his writings. Furthermore, his gods seem to be nothing more than natural forces."[5] Take also the view of Aristotle. At times his god is the immanent principle of the universe,[6] but generally he conceives of him as dwelling in a supramundane calm. He is concerned only with himself, exists in a state of self-contemplation. Hence he becomes for men merely an ideal state, and the personal element is gone.[7]

In the case of Stoicism, which was the dominant philosophy in the first century of our era, the same situation obtains. God is spoken of as the Logos, and as Fire from which all things came and to which all things return. Generally that ultimate something is not conceived of in any personal sense. The Stoics do speak of Reason as lord, and even as Father at times, but again this is matched by other expressions such as Fate and Fortune which destroys the effectiveness of the utterance. There are occasional references in Marcus Aurelius to a personal God, but usually he does not express himself in that way.[8]

One means of testing a view is to observe its working and result. Now if one takes the pains to investigate how many of these Stoics seemed to be quite satisfied with their own system, the outcome is very disheartening. If this God were so near and good and powerful, why were so many Stoics driven to suicide? Surely a system which fails to give courage to endure has a very wide breach in its walls. The trouble, among

---

4. By demons are meant not wicked spirits, but supernatural beings.
5. Demos. R.: Philosophy of Plato p. 100.
6. Cf. Meta. 982a-983a25; Ethics 1178b 26-1179a30.
7. Mercier, L. J.: The Challenge of Humanism p. 33.
8. M. Aurelius: Med. IV, 40; V, 8.

other things, lay here that the abstractions of the mind gave no final satisfaction in the stress of life. And the cause was that the vital element of approach to and contact with a living personality was missing.

It is hardly necessary to point out that in both the Old and the New Testaments it is exactly this which means everything to the faithful. To be sure there are other elements which reenforced this fundamental view. God is love, as well as power and intelligence; He rules the world with a kindly providence; He is distinct from the world as well as in it. All these elements will be discussed in the following chapters. It is sufficient here to point out that this fundamental that God is indeed a living person and is Father in a most vital way differs widely from any view held by pagan antiquity. It bridges the gap between God and man without doing away, as Stoicism did, with the distinction of the two. The perfect prayer addresses God as Our Father who art in heaven. Intimate relation but also infinite separation. Compare with that the high sentiment of Plato that "to find the maker and father of the universe is a task and to declare him to all after one has found him is impossible."[9] Here we have a God exalted but far beyond man's grasp. Christianity teaches an exalted God but one very near at the same time.

Another essential difference in the view of God to which attention should be called is the unique emphasis in the Old and the New Testaments that there is only one God. The emphatic words of Moses resound throughout the pages of Scripture: "Hear, O Israel, Jehovah our God is one Jehovah."[10] God is absolutely supreme in wisdom, righteousness, power, holiness, mercy. He rules sovereign over all. The teaching of Scripture is that of genuine montheism.

Every one knows that the Graeco-Roman world was peopled with many gods. The populace brought sacrifice and adoration to each and all. But among the thinkers there was a

---

9. Timaeus 28c
10. Deut. 6:4.

sharp criticism both of the practices of the individual gods and of the many deities as such. It must be admitted that the general course of thought was toward one supreme being, or rather one supreme something. But it is going altogether too far to maintain that monotheistic conceptions were prevalent. Much less is it correct to maintain, as some have done, that Stoicism is a monotheistic system.

As an example I would point to an interpretation of a passage quoted from Marcus Aurelius. The words, "There is one universe, one God, immanent in all things, one substance, one law, one reason common to all intelligent creatures, and one truth," are given as a parallel to the statement in Paul, "yet to us there is one God, the Father, of whom are all things, and we unto him; and one Lord Jesus Christ, through whom are all things, and we through him." [11]

The trouble here lies in using words very carelessly. Monotheism is first shorn of its real meaning, namely that there is one absolutely supreme spiritual being. Then confusion is made between monotheism and monism, as though the two were identical. And after that it is declared that the Scripture and Stoicism teach the same thing on this point.

The difference ought to be clearly seen by all. The grain of truth in saying that monotheism was held by pagan antiquity is that there was a tendency in both literature and philosophy toward the recognition of one will, the will of Zeus. They often did see that there must be some one unifying principle. But just as soon as one seeks to know more definitely the character of that ultimate something, the contrast between Christian and pagan thought is clear. Certainly one cannot ascribe to it the attributes of the One God of the Scriptures.

Finally, God according to the Scripture is spirit. The long course of the history of Israel had emphasized it. No one of the writers of the New Testament taught differently. The Old Testament emphasized that God is immaterial. Jehovah

---

11. I Cor. 8:6; Gilbert, G. H.: *Greek Thought in the New Testament*, p. 64.

is the "I am that I am."   God Means to the writers of the
New Testament a spiritual Being.   God is Spirit.[12]

When we compare this with Stoicism we find a strong
contrast.   The ultimate substance there lacks both personality
and spirituality.   Repeatedly the Stoics speak of the primal
substance as fire, and that is God.   This is why that element
will finally also consume all things, and all will return to the
original being.

Both Christianity and Stoicism agree that there is an ultimate substance.   But when the simple question is put as to the
character of that substance, the answer is totally different.
If monotheism connotes anything in the light of the New
Testament it is that God is a spiritual personality.   Stoicism
has neither an ultimate spirit nor an ultimate personality.
For this fiery primal substance is everywhere, in man, the
material universe, the heavenly bodies.   This is the all-pervad-
ing divinity.   Listen to Cicero: "A similar argument can be
used to prove that the world is wise, happy, and eternal; for
things possessed of each of these attributes are superior to
things devoid of them, and nothing is superior to the world.
From this it will follow that the world is god."[13]   And later
Seneca says: "These ancient sages recognized the same Jupiter as we do, the guardian and ruler of the universe, its soul
and breath, the maker and lord of this earthly frame of things,
to whom every name of power is appropriate.   If you prefer
to call him fate you will not be wrong.   He it is on whom
depend all things, from whom proceed all causes of causes.
If you prefer to call him providence you will still be right;
for he it is by whose counsel provision is made for the world
that it may pursue its orderly course and unfold the drama of
its being.   If you prefer to call him nature, you will make
no mistake; for it is he from whom all things derive being
and by whose breath we live.   If you prefer to call him the
world, you will not be in error for he is everything that you

---

12. John 4:24.
13. Cicero: De Nat. Deor. II, VIII, 21.

can see; he is totally infused in all his parts, self-sustained through inherent power."[14] A transcendent God such as Christianity teaches Stoicism does not have. The best that can be said for Stoicism is that it is monistic and pantheistic. Monotheistic it is by no means.

14. Seneca; Natur. Quaest. II, 45.

CHAPTER VIII

God and the Logos

It is Not the writer's intention to enter in this chapter on a discussion of the specifically theological question concerning the relation of God the Father and Jesus Christ the Son in the Holy Trinity. The object is rather to give a specific content to the term Logos. Through doing that something will be seen of the nature of the second person in the Trinity. The Gospel of St. John[1] speaks very clearly about the Logos. It is because it has repeatedly been stated that the idea as we find it expressed in John has its origin in Greek thought and is quite identical with it that the task is imposed upon us. The purpose is therefore to examine the teaching of John quite carefully and to compare it with the conception of Heracleitus, the Stoics, and Philo Judaeus.

It is very evident that there was a teaching concerning "Logos" beginning with Heracleitus and continuing through Greek literature. But again the question must be stated as not being whether the word "Logos" was used repeatedly, but whether the content put into that word was identical, or nearly so. For that exactly is the contention of those who would have Christianity evolve from the religious, social, philosophical, and ethical conceptions of the Graeco-Roman world.

Before we undertake to examine the relation of the two concepts, we must pause to look at the word itself. John writes, "In the beginning was the Logos and the Logos was with God and the Logos was God."[2] Now it is extremely interesting to note that there is no word in English nor German,

---

1. St. John 1:1-8.
2. John 1:1.

nor even in Latin which accurately and adequately gives the meaning of the word "Logos". We translate it as the "Word," but will see shortly why this is only part of its meaning. The Latin Christians debated as to which of the three words Verbum, Sermo, or Ratio was the nearest equivalent. Though not entirely satisfied they ultimately decided on Verbum only. Tertullian uses Sermo and Ratio together to represent the Greek word.[3] Origen has the same difficulty with the word for he writes "He who honors the Son, who is the Word and Reason."[4] When the Latins decided on Verbum they thereby deprived the word Logos of half its meaning. And to a Greek the half left out was the more important half.

For "Logos" contains two elements, "speech" and "reason." The one designates the vocal utterance while the other emphasizes the thought contained in the utterance. The Greek meant by Logos especially the latter. Logos was the idea, the thought the reason expressing itself in an utterance, or in fact in anything. Possibly the meaning can be made clearer by a reference to the Platonic dialogues. There it repeatedly occurs in the argument that Socrates is asked or asks of the interlocutor "What do you say." But the thought is not that the words have not been heard, but rather the inquiry is about the meaning of the words heard. The question then is "What is the thought that you are advancing." That of course is the verb form linked up with the noun Logos. But the noun had the same meaning for the Greek. Throughout Greek literature it is "Logos" that lies at the bottom of things. It is Logos through which things are what they are. That being the case it can readily be seen that any word which in the first place suggests oral, vocal utterance does not convey what the Greek word means. And the Latin word Verbum does precisely that.

---

3. Apol. 21.
4. *Contra Celsum,* Bk. VIII, Chap. IX.

Now in the Old Testament the "Word of the Lord" is often spoken of in the sense of being related to the creation of things. In Genesis we read "And God said, Let there be, and there was." In the Psalms we read "Through the Word of the Lord were the heavens made."[5] The Hebrew undoubtedly thought of the "Word" as the vocal utterance, which called things into being, and not as the thought or reason inherent in them. Thus the Hebrew and the Greek in their thinking were at opposite poles. The one regards the Word as above and outside the created world; the other as immanent and residing in it.

It is Philo the Jew who tried to harmonize generally the thought of these two nations. He both Mosaizes Greek thought and Hellenizes Hebrew thought. What he did in the case of the "Logos" will be seen a little later. The point arrived at thus far is that the Greek and the Hebrew, though both recognized that "Logos" was bound up with the nature of things, yet had a totally different thought in mind when they gave meaning to "Logos."

The early Greek philosopher Heracleitus made a great deal of the Logos. What then did he mean by the term? Not at all what the Hebrew meant when he spoke of the Word. For the latter presupposed a personal transcendent God, high above his creation and the sole cause of it. The Word then proceeded from God and was his utterance. But such an idea Heracleitus did not, and in fact could not hold. For if there is the Word of God, there must be the God who speaks. And exactly that Heracleitus nowhere teaches. He does not affirm the existence of a transcendent God. Therefore Logos could not mean for him the "Word." As a forerunner of later intellectuals among the Greeks, Heracleitus understands by Logos the reason or thought underlying and inherent in particulars. It is the immanent Reason in the world, conceived of as both material and spiritual. Here we already see the typically Greek conception of the world as an ordered, ration-

5. Psalm 33:6.

al something. And that which gives it this character is Logos.

In the further development of Greek thought the Word is supplanted by another. From Anaxagoras on the word in common use is Nous (Mind). But the fundamental idea is the same. In all things Mind or Reason is operating and expressing itself. In Plato and Aristotle we find this same view. But in the Stoics the word Logos again came to the fore. They conceived of Logos in a two-fold manner. At one time it is the unspoken thought, or in the case of man the inner psychical function. Again the Logos was conceived of by them as expressing itself in word or in act. The distinction was brought out by the terms logos endiathetos in the first instance, and logos prophorikos in the second. Now Philo, the Jew of Alexandria, spoke of the Logos in both senses. At one time Logos signifies to him the immanent reason, present in the world, and containing within itself the world-ideal. But at other times the Logos is viewed from the other point of view. It then is the word spoken by God, proceeding from Him, issuing from Him, and creating the world. In Philo then both the Hebrew and the Greek meaning is attached to the word. The Stoic spoke of the "spermatic word," and Philo linked up the Old Testament conception of the "Word of the Lord" with the Stoic view. The Word is then conceived by Philo as the rational and spiritual principle immanent in both man and the universe, and again he lifted it above and outside the universe so that it becomes a kind of mediator between the Absolute, the Ultimate, God, and the created world.

To understand clearly the difference between this view of Philo and that of St. John it is necessary to examine the Logos teaching of the latter. John ascribes to the Logos the following characteristics. It is preexistent, in fact John's statement[6] denotes absolute existence. Of all other things

---

6. John 1:1.

it is said that they "became," and also the Word "became" flesh. But Logos existed before all created things, and also before the incarnation. It was in that same relation to men, and hence became the source of light. Therefore Justin Martyr says of it "The Logos was made flesh in Christ, but while the Christians possess as it were the entire Logos, yet fragments of the Logos, sporadic manifestations of Him are scattered through the heathen world. There the activity of the Logos has been displayed in the philosophers, poets, and lawgivers."[7] The Logos existed but also resided in the souls of men.

Further John declares that the Logos was a Divine Person. That it is divine is evident from the statement "And the Word was God." The thought of John that the Word is a person requires a little elucidation. The Greek which is translated "and the Word was with God" indicates this clearly. The expression, a prepositional phrase, is used in the New Testament to convey the idea of a living union and communion. It implies, therefore, the notion of active intercourse. Hence what John states, means that the Word was not merely coexistent with God so that the two might be contemplated separately as in a merely local relation, but that the Personal Being of the Word was in active intercourse with God. There is between the two a perfect communion.

This Logos is also transcendent. It existed before any other thing, and all things were created through it. There are no intermediate beings in the thought of John. Rather there is a direct relation between him who is God, and the world which is created. For John does not postulate the eternity of matter, nor does he conceive of it as having come into existence through beings inferior to God.

If one then compares this conception of the Logos with that of pure Greek thought, or even with the Hellenized thought of Philo, the two are evidently quite different. For Heracleitus conceives of the Logos only as the source of being,

7. I Apol. 5:46; cf. II Apol. 8:10.

the life energy, or the cause or reason for things being what they are. The distinct features of Eternal, Personal, Divine, Transcendent existence are not ascribed to his Logos. In the case of Philo there is no explicit teaching that the Logos was preexistent, nor is it coexistent with the eternal God. The Logos is a being inferior to the august Absolute. And Philo has also hellenized so much that he at times postulates eternal matter, whereas John declares that through the Logos the world was created. Heracleitus knows the Logos only as the immanent principle of rationality in the uinverse, and nowhere does it attain the height of personality. He gives it a certain universality but it remains impersonal. Throughout Greek thought runs the same concept. Never would he even have dared to identify it with a human personality as is done by John. Philo is not consistent in the meaning attached to the Logos. He shifts from the genuinely Hebrew one of Word to the Greek one of Reason. As the Reason of God he regards the Logos as immanent in the world and as being an element or phase of the Absolute Being. But when he views the Logos as the "Word" of God he treats it as distinct person. However, the best that can be said of Philo is that his meaning is vague and not clearly distinquished. Hardly too, is the Logos truly divine. For his exaltation of the Absolute God makes it impossible to conceive of God as having direct contact with finite creation. That would contaminate his divine essence. To account for the relation of God to the world inferior beings must be interposed. The Logos is such a being, and therefore is not absolutely divine. It stands on the border-line between Creator and Creation. It is neither like God nor like men. Midway between, it becomes an Ambassador from the Ruler to his subjects, and conversely is a suppliant from mortal men to God.[8] The most concise statement from Philo is this: "The Father, who has begotten all things, granted as his choicest privilege to his chief messenger and most august Logos, that

---

8. Leg. Alleg. 3:62.

he should stand in the midst between the Creator and the created. Now he is, on the one hand always the suppliant for transient mortals in the presence of the Immortal, and the Ambassador of the Ruler to his subject. Thus he rejoices because of the privilege, and prides himself on it — being neither uncreated like God nor created like you, but standing between the two extremes as a pledge to both, to him who created as an assurance that created beings will never wholly rebel or revolt, choosing confusion rather than order, and in the case of the creature to give him the bright hope that the gracious God will never ignore his own work."[9]

Philo was thoroughly acquainted with the Old Testament writings. Yet his Hellenism led him into a vague doctrine of the Logos. He has retained something of the Hebrew teaching, but in the main has departed from it. The teaching of John is a further development in the same line as the Old Testament, and retains therefore the distinctive elements of the Absoluteness of the Logos, completely other than the world, externally existent, through whom all things were created. And the crowning thought is that this Logos which is very God took on human form in order to bring about the redemption of the world. This element, the soteriological, is completely absent from Philo.

The argument thus far has been negative. We have attempted to show that the source of this Logos doctrine is not to be found in Greek philosophy. Whence then did it come? Was there any other source from which it might have sprung? Assuredly, for among the Jews there was a mass of wisdom literature in which the Logos idea occupied a prominent place. And we regard it as much more probable that the fully developed doctrine in John and Paul, though less clearly stated by the latter, was linked up with the idea as it had already

---

9. Quis Rerum Divinarum Heres sit. 205.

been developed in this Wisdom literature.[10] Philo may have contributed to the terminology employed in the statements about the Logos.   Extremely interesting are his reference to the Logos as the first born, the image, and the bond of the universe.[11]

---

10. Harris, R.: Origin of the Prologue in John's Gospel. p. 28.
11. Philo: De Specialibus Legibus I 81; De Confusione 146, 147; De Fuga 101, 112; De Somniis I 215; idem II 45.

CHAPTER VIII

God and the World

A FURTHER point of comparison of the views of the Graeco-Roman world and Christianity is the relation of God to the world. One can already draw conclusions from the statements made in the two preceding chapters. The conception of God present in the two views will necessarily determine what is held to be the relation between God and the world. On this point again we find a wide divergence. The Greeks of old had contemplated the world in its beauty, its power, its order. Keen observation of its detailed operations had been carried on, but also prolonged discussion of its origin and nature. Whence then did this universe come?

The answer in Genesis is that it was brought about by the fiat of God. The doctrine of creation is written on almost every page of both Testaments. Specifically, John assigns the work of creation to the Logos. Clearly he states that all things were made through Him and without Him nothing was made that was made. Preceding that was eternity when the Word was with God. The world was not and was called into being through the Logos of God.

One looks in vain for such a view in Greek and Roman literature. Because the Greek had a peculiar conception of matter (to be discussed in chapter XII) it was a foregone conclusion that he would not accept the creation of matter out of nothing by God. In fact he never supposed that God could create the universe. That he did so is explicitly denied by Heracleitus, Empedocles, and Anaxagoras. Among the Romans Lucretius says, "and her (nature's) first principle we will derive from this that no thing is ever by divine power produced from nothing."[1]

How then explain its existence? Because he held to a materialistic conception of God, his world and God are in many cases identical. But where such is not the case it is postulated that matter is eternal. The only creation the Greek then knows is the bringing into order and system of this original chaotic mass. No Greek thinker held to a divine creation ex nihilo.[2] According to Hesiod the gods on Mt. Olympus did not create the world, but merely govern it after it has been created by natural forces. Thus too Anaxagoras presents it. It is reason which orders all things, and makes a cosmos out of chaos. After this has been done the world continues of itself. Due to the presence of the element of reason in the world it is what it is automatically. In the Sophist[3] Plato puts into the mouth of the Eleatic stranger the thought of an absolute creation, but in the Timaeus[4] he says, "He brought it into order out of disorder, deeming that the former state is in all ways better than the latter." The view of Aristotle is as follows. The idea of God for Aristotle is pure idea. God lives in perfect contemplation of himself alone. He needs the world in no way and the world is eternal.[5]

The teaching of the Bible plainly indicates that though God has created the world He is at the same time quite distinct from it. He is not identified with the world so that the two become one. God is in heaven and in a very real sense apart from the world. The teaching of both the Old and the New Testaments is that God is immanent and at the same time transcendent with reference to His creation. At this point

1. Lucretius: De Nat. Rer. I. 149-150.
2. McClure, M. J.: Greek Conception of Nature. Phil. Rev. Mar. 1934.
3. Sophist 265c.
4. Timaeus 30a.
5. Meta. 1072a-1076a, especially 1072a7-12, 1074b10-12; cf. De Caelo 279b-283b22.

also the contrast between the Scripture teaching and that of the Graeco-Roman world is very specific.

For the thing which characterizes the latter is exactly this that the element of transcendence is denied. The whole train of thought of both the Greeks and the Romans is in the direction of immanence. An apparent exception is Plato. And yet it is only apparent. Plato does lay emphasis on the existence of a supersensual world which is the real world. The idea of the Good stands above everything, but the weakness of Plato's view is that there is no personal God. Plato's conception of the supersensuous world has always made the church feel a certain kinship with Platonism. However, the vital, all important element of genuine personality as taught by Christianity is lacking. Heracleitus taught that fire was the ultimate substance, and this pervaded the whole universe. In the case of Stoicism the Logos constituted an ethereal substance, akin to fire but more refined and subtle, and also more mobile. This was present in man, and all the world of nature. The two are therefore identical. And with identification the possibility of transcendence is gone.

This doctrine of immanence as taught by Stoicism is recognized by St. Paul in his speech on the Areopagus.[6] Seneca presents some very close parallels to the teaching of Paul, e. g. "the whole world is the temple of the immortal gods."[7] and especially the following: "God is near thee; He is with thee; He is within."[8] Cicero also teaches the same thing: "Hence it follows that the world possesses wisdom, and that the element which holds all things in its embrace is preeminently and perfectly rational, and therefore that the world is god, and all the forces of the world are held together by the divine nature."[9]

If one examines this teaching of Stoicism it becomes evident that even in the case of the doctrine of immanence the

---

6. Acts 17:21 ff; cf. Rom. 11:36.
7. *De Benef.* VII, 7.
8. Ep. Mor. 41:1.
9. De Nat. Deor. II. XI, 30; cf. II, XIV, 39; II, VIII, 21.

emphasis is different from what we find in Christian teaching. The Stoic Seneca, puts it in this way that God is in us. Although Christianity states it thus at times, the prevailing way is the opposite. God is not in us, but we are in God through Jesus Christ. The view of Stoicism stresses identification with the divine, while Christianity adheres strictly to the thought that God transcends us although we are in intimate fellowship with Him. Further evidence of the difference will be given in the discussion of the nature of man.

A further point of interest in the discussion of God's relation to the world lies in the idea of "providence." It is often presented that the Stoic belief in providence was a forerunner of and identical with the Christian teaching. First of all it is interesting to note that the New Testament uses the word pronoia but twice, while the Stoics frequently employ the term. Thus Aurelius says, "Full of Providence are the works of the gods, nor are Fortune's works independent of Nature or of the woven texture and interlacement of all that is under the control of Providence."[10] The fact is also that in the two passages Acts 24:2 and Romans 13:14 the word does not have the meaning which we attach to Providence. Yet the New Testament is replete with the idea of Providence, and that a Providence far richer than the Stoics'. Specific passages such as Matt. 6:26-34 and 10:29-31 illustrate the idea that every detail in the life of God's children is the object of his perfect knowledge and love.

The Stoic speaks of Providence in the sense of the general design in the universe, of the fitness of part to the whole but apparently it is none too definite nor too gracious. The Christian teaching is that everything is perfectly determined and secure with the Father who knows all things and loves his children with a perfect love. Seneca, however, says that the gods "are supreme commanders in the universe, controlling all things by their power and acting as guardians of the human race, even though they are sometimes unmindful of the

---

10. Med. XII, 1; cf. II, 3.

individual."[11]   Cicero says, "The gods care for great things but neglect the little,"[12] and "according to the Stoic doctrine, the gods are not directly responsible for every fissure in the liver or for every song of a bird, since, manifestly, that would not be seemly or proper in a god and furthermore is impossible."[13]   This was an echo of Euripides that god "will intervene in matters grown too great, but small things he lets pass and leaves to Fate."[14]   Epictetus expresses the same sentiment.[15]   Note the contrast with the expression that not a hair of one's head shall perish.[16]   In the teaching of the New Testament the individual stands out as of great importance.   Not merely the general course of things is the object of Providence but even the minutest detail.   The Stoic, however, must be in an uncertain frame of mind.   Is he or is he not the object of divine care?

Furthermore, the effect of the Stoic belief in Providence is undermined or nullified by contrary teachings.   Not only was there Providence, but also Fate or Chance.   And of Fortune Cicero writes, "Who fails to comprehend the enormous twofold power of Fortune for weal and for woe?"[17]   Seneca says, "We have come into the realm of Fortune, and harsh and invincible is her power, things deserved and undeserved must we suffer just as she wills.   With violence, insult and cruelty she will maltreat our bodies."[18]   The good effect that the belief in Providence had was thus offset by the belief in Chance or Fate.   The contrast between Stoicism and Christianity on this point is absolute.   Fortune and Fate appear repeatedly in the Stoic writings but not once does either word occur in the New Testament.   Providence in the New Testament is real; Providence according to the Stoic may be

---

11. Seneca: Ep. XCV, 50.
12. Cicero: De Nat. Deor. II, 167.
13. idem: De Divinatione I, LII, 118.
14. Euripides: Fr. 974.
15. Epictetus: Disc. I, XII, 1; cf. Aurelius' Med. VI, 44.
16. Luke 21:18.
17. Cicero: De Officiis II, VI, 19.
18. Seneca: Ad Marciam X, 6: cf. Ad Polyb. XVI, 4; Ad Helviam V, 4.

eclipsed by Chance at any moment. Epictetus says, "Surrender everything to the Deity, to Fortune."[19] Dread fear, therefore, hangs over the Stoic. Seneca wrote, "When you are about to rejoice most, you will have most to fear. When everything seems to you to be peaceful, the forces that will harm you are not non-existent, but inactive. Always believe that there will come some blow to strike you."[20] The peace of God that passeth all understanding is the Christians possession.

The evidence that the Stoic doctrine of Providence is not of the same substance as the Christian should be evident further from its effect. A vague general belief in the control of the universe, which at the same time leaves one in the lurch through the sudden intrusion of Chance, cannot serve as a buoy to tried souls. That is why the Stoic so repeatedly says that the way is open when things become unbearable. That too is why the Stoic so readily made use of the "open door." You can always pull out of the situation that overwhelms you with its evil. The Stoic thereby maintained his vaunted mastery over circumstances, but at the same time admitted that kindly Providence had forsaken him.

By contrast the Christian belief maintains that loving care is behind and through it all. That being the case, there is no question of suicide. But the Stoic openly advocated it. Many of the leaders took their own lives. This was because Fortune, Fate occupied the place of kindly Providence in their lives. Such a possibility the Christian does not admit. Since the Christian believes that everything affecting his life is subservient to an Almighty Love, and an all-knowing Father who cares for him in perfect love, he gains a unique spiritual repose, and unruffled calm. The Stoic seeks to cultivate and gain a supreme indifference to the evils which befall him. He looks beyond the particulars and sees the universal and the universe, controlled by intelligence and not by love. The Christian sees

19. Disc. IV, 4, 39.
20. De Ira II, XXXI, 5.

even the most insignificant in the light of a personal God who
is love. Seneca states the Stoic position as follows: "What
is the duty of a good man? To resign himself to his destiny.
It is a great consolation to share the fate of the universe.
Whatever it be that decrees how we are to live, how to die,
it binds even the gods by the same inexorable law."[21] The
Stoic at best rests in a cold Universal; the Christian in infinite warmth of love.

Closely allied to the idea of providence is the conception
of the course of history. The view of the Greeks and Romans
is quite different from what is given in the Old and New
Testaments. Among the Greeks the course of history is
viewed either as a process of degeneration or as a recurrent
cycle. The classic example of the former is found in Hesiod.[22]
Throughout the literature there are frequent allusions to the
golden age which once was but has progressively deteriorated
until the present. The eye is turned longingly toward that
glorious past characterized by simplicity and innocence.
Poetic souls were haunted by its charm, and pictured it in
its idyllic relations.

The philosophic souls looked upon history as a cycle. The
world of men went through successive stages of progressive
civilization and then of degeneration. After a time the universe reverted to its original form and thereafter the same
would repeat itself. History was exactly duplicated in every
detail. The doctrine of progress which became almost a
fetich in the latter half of the nineteenth and the first decade
of the twentieth century was not known to classical antiquity.
Nowhere is there that bland optimism, which blindly believed
that human affairs were ever proceeding along the path of
advance to higher levels of more beautiful, true, and good
living among men. It cannot be said, on the other hand, that
pessimism characterized the outlook. The ultimate end was
cause for neither optimism nor pessimism. The course of

---

21. De Prov. V, 6.
22. *Work and Days,* 109-201.

events goes in a cycle which again reproduces what had been before. The view reminds strongly of the wheel-of-existence philosophy of India. This view which originated among the Greeks was so prevalent as to be regarded the normal, almost orthodox view. From them it passed on to the Romans.[23]

Plato contemplates the world cycle as consisting of 36,000 solar years. For half that length of time the creator guides the affairs of the universe. Thereafter he relaxes his hold and a period of progressive degeneration sets in.[24] Aristotle views civilization in the same way. He declares that "every art and philosophy has probably been repeatedly developed to the utmost and has perished again."[25]

The glance of the Stoic was essentially backward. Idealizing the past he put forth efforts and held high hopes of restoring the simplicity of the ages gone by.[26] He too held to a cyclic view of history. It repeats itself to the minutest detail. Aurelius wrote, "The same upwards, downwards from cycle to cycle are the revolutions of the universe."[27] Specifically he says, "The rational soul wanders round the whole world and through the encompassing void, and gazes into infinite time, and considers the periodic destructions and re-births of the universe, and reflects that our posterity will see nothing new, and that our ancestors have seen nothing greater than we have seen."[28]

By contrast the teaching of the New Testament is ever looking forward. Throughout its pages the glad tidings of the ultimate victory of the Kingdom of God is proclaimed. The Christian belief presents a cataclysmic end, but what a different one from that of Stoicism which taught that at the end of the cycle the world was again reduced by a general conflagration to its primal fiery state. After that a new cycle

---

23. Cf. Virgil: Fourth Eclogue.
24. Pol. 269e-274d; Tim. 39d; Rep. 546.
25. Meta. 1074b10; cf. De Caelo 270b16-20.
26. Med. XI, 1; VI, 37: VI, 46; VII, 1.
27. Med. IX, 28; cf. X, 7; Seneca Ad Marcian XXI, 2; XXVI, 6.
28. Med. XI. 1.

in which the events, the persons are again identical with what had been in previous cycles.[29] So universal was this conflagration that even the souls of the wise would be absorbed by it. But Christianity, as did Israel,[30] teaches that events are moving toward an end which is truly the end. Through all the circumstances and events of the world-history a true Providence is working with perfect design. It too believes in a general conflagration which will reduce all things in the physical world. And after that? Not the same, but a new world. After the conflagration a new heaven and a new earth in which dwelleth righteousness. From that world all the imperfections, all the sin-stained and sin-marred is gone forever. At the rebirth[31] of all things that which appears is totally different in character from what was before. And that other world abides forever.

29. Cicero: De Nat. Deor. II, 46; Seneca: Epist. I, 9, 16.
30. Cf. Berdyaev, N.: Meaning of History p. 28.
31. Matt. 19:28.

CHAPTER IX

God and Man

THE CONTENT of this chapter looks at the relation of God and man from the opposite point of view from what was taken previously. There the emphasis fell on the relation of God to the world. Here it is the relation of the world of men to God, or more specifically the worship of God.

The very concept of the religious life possesses for us a content different from what it had for the ancient Greeks and Romans. To us true religion is unthinkable without certain very elemental factors. It suggests immediately a definite set of doctrines which are formulated in a creed. Again it implies an organization, the church, which supports, defends, and propagates the elements of its creed. And too, religion suggests such an organization as existing more or less independent of the state.

Now the religion of the Greeks included none of these things. There was no formulation of beliefs in a creed. There was no church which professed acceptance of these beliefs, and the urgent call to propagate them. There was therefore no demand on him who professed himself religious to accept these beliefs. There was no conception of an authoritative book which spoke with finality on the matters of faith and practice. The individual who today is a genuine son of the Reformation has but to call before his consciousness the essential content of his personal religion to realize that there is the widest possible gap between him and the ancient pagan of both Greece and Rome. But in the case of some denominational beliefs and practices he will observe very near approaches to what obtained in pagan antiquity. Let him muse on the emphasis on ritual, the lack of definite beliefs, the ignoring of any individual acceptance of them, as is manifest in many liberal churches today, and he will clearly see the difference. The basic elements in the philosophy of religion are entirely different.

First of all there was an absolute identification of religion and state. Hence the emphasis in the religious life fell on duly prescribed ritualistic performances, which were carried out as part of the life of the state. The Greek religion was primarily a matter of practice, but not of belief. By practice is not meant what it might suggest to many, i.e. that their religion had to be carried out in their lives, in their conduct. Rather it simply means that the religious life expressed itself in official ritualistic performance and not in accepted propositions.

The contrast on this point with genuine Christianity is very great. For if Christianity stresses any one thing it surely is that all depends upon what the individual himself is and believes. All true manifestations of the church are one on this point. The thing that counts is the inner state of the soul and its individual relation to God. This view was completely foreign to most ancients. How could it be otherwise in view of their conception of the gods? They were superior to men in strength, in stature, in wisdom, but no excellence in moral and spiritual attributes was assigned to them. The relations to the gods are therefore not conceived of on the level of morals, but on that of certain deeds. Religious life expressed itself in ritualistic sacrifice, in presenting costly gifts, in processions in their honor. This doing things as a service to the gods had a very wide application. The games and the contests, physical and intellectual, were included. Hence, running, boxing, the reading of poetry in contests, the rendition of the drama, received a religious character. Performance of the ritual or participation in it was considered ground for benefits. Thus at the beginning of the Iliad we have this view expressed

by the priest Chryses.[1] Again Agamemnon reproaches Zeus
for the disaster brought upon him, although he had made sacrifice upon every altar.[2] So failure to bring sacrifice might
bring disaster.[3]

A corollary of this emphasis on ritual is the fact that instruction, admonition, and reproof find no place. The New
Testament everywhere evidences a real interest in the defense
and propagation of its doctrines. It would have men become
grounded and settled in the truth. But since the Greeks had
no officially accepted mythology, there could be no formal instruction in it as a thing to be believed. In fact it was not
regarded as a sin to disbelieve the mythological tales, but it
was a grievous thing not to take part ritually in the official
state religion.

In the later development in both the Mystery religions and
Stoicism there is a slightly different emphasis. The Mysteries
did make a formal, ritualistic appeal to purity. But even there
the emphasis was not on doctrine. The whole thrust lay in
the ritual which was to be believed in and practised. In the
case of Stoicism the emphasis shifts much more to the inner
attitude of the individual. Previously the ritual was everything. The founder of Stoicism, Zeno, criticized the exter-
nalism and ritualism of their worship. He states that images,
shrines, sacrifice, prayers and worship are of no avail. The
best thing, says he, is to reverence the gods with a pure and
sincere mind. Seneca later speaks in exactly the same vein.
"God is to be worshipped not by sacrifice and much bloodshed
— for what pleasure has he in the slaughter of innocent victims — but by a pure heart, a good and honorable purpose.
No lofty temples of stone should be erected to him; he is to be
worshipped in each man's own soul."[4] Another quotation
from Seneca emphasize the point. He writes "Not even in
victims, though they be fat and their brows glitter with gold,

1. Il. I, 37-41.
2. Il. VIII, 236 ff.
3. Od. IV, 351. ff.
4. Fragment 123; cf. Epist. 95, 47-50; 115, 5.

is honor paid to the gods, but in the pious and upright intent of the worshippers."[5] The lame philosopher Epictetus says the same thing.[6]

The explanation of this change in the case of Stoicism is not difficult. If one but remembers the origin and the stronghold of Stoicism it becomes very clear. For though Stoicism took root in Athens (in fact gets its name from the Painted Porch there) and flourished in Rome, it is not really a philosophy of the Graeco-Roman world. Its origins are in the Orient, and many of its leaders were Orientals of a Semitic stamp. Therefore they emphasized the individual and personal element in their religious views.

The fact has already been mentioned that the religious life was conceived of by the Greeks as public. In fact it was regarded much more as a social and political thing than an individual matter. The same view obtained among the Romans. Man's attachment to the divine was rooted in his corporate life. He was a member of a household, of a tribe, of a city. This city, tribe, and household had its gods and goddesses. To them he was bound and obligated, not so much as an individual, but as member of these larger groups through his very birth in them. Especially in Greece in the hey-day of the city-state was this the case. But after the city-state had begun to disappear under Philip of Macedon and later under Alexander the Great we do note an increase of individualism also in religion. It continues when the Greek cities have fallen prey to the Roman eagle. As the sense of being one member of a comparatively small body decreased, the individual was thrown back upon himself for "the political developments of the Hellenistic Age had changed the conception of the state from the body in which each member played its part into a body in which the head was the all-important matter."[7] But in the fifth century the identification of the religious life with

5. De Benef. I. 6.
6. Dis. I. 16.
7. Knox W.: St. Paul and the Church of the Gentiles p. 161.

that of the state was complete, and the state was the supreme end. Thus Gilbert Murray has characterized the situation in the words, "the real religion was a devotion to the city itself."[8] By contrast Christianity makes devotion to God himself the highest goal.

This overemphasis of the state and its demands as over against the individual can be made clear also by the example of the position occupied by the priests. There was a strong tendency to make them subordinate to the magistrates. At least they were appointed as state officials. The temples too were state property, built and maintained by money supplied by the state. Again religious law was administered by the state courts. In every respect religion and the state are one. Accordingly Plato lays down the law that private religion and worship is generally to be prohibited.[9]

A third characteristic of Greek religion is its emphasis on the beautiful. Throughout the artistic plays a very large part. Because it stressed the ritualistic and public character of worship it was to be expected that their religion would be one of the beautiful. The elements which appealed to and had an effect on the worshipper were not the lofty religious teachings about God and his nature and will. Nor was it the appeal of noble morality in its purity. What drew the Greek was that which appealed to the eye. The beautiful pomp of the stately processions, the gorgeous temples in their perfection of symmetry and proportion, the marvelous mythological scenes immortalized in relief, the exquisitely wrought statues of men, heroes, and gods, glistening in gold and ivory, and the splendor of the ritual of sacrifice. Every element had to contribute its part toward making the whole beautiful. Artistic forms were the real means of elevating the worshipper.

It is highly important to note clearly the difference between Christianity and the Greek religion on this point. For immediately the question arises whether the Christian religion

---

8. Murray G.; *Five Stages of Greek Religion* p. 98.
9. Plato; *Laws* 909.

does not employ the beautiful as well as the Greek. The answer would be both negative and positive. For surely the Christian religion would use the beautiful in the worship of the one and only God. The difference between the two is one of emphasis. Probably the best way to clarify the point is to take an example from the Old Testament. For the fundamentals of the religious life as given there have passed over into the New Testament.

The Hebrew worshipped God in the beauty of holiness. The Greek worshipped his gods in beauty. The one finds expression of the religious life in the fields of morals, of ethics, of the will. Holiness as conceived of in God was on the one hand separation from all that which was tainted by sin and on the other the expression of the perfectly good. The major emphasis in the case of the Hebrew falls on this concept of holiness. The emphasis with the Greek falls on the concept of beauty. The Greek soul reacted to something first of all in the realm of the aesthetic; the Hebrew in that of the moral. The Greek ideal of man was that of kalagathia. But note carefully that the concept of the beautiful comes first. This the Hebrew reverses. But the two views are not mutually exclusive. Rather the fact is that the Hebrew has the fuller and richer conception. Holiness came first and was also a beautiful thing. The Greek placed beauty first, and did not associate it with or bind it to the idea of holiness. The Hebrew worshipped in holiness expressing itself in beauty. The Greek saw only the beauty and was indifferent to its moral character. If this distinction between the two peoples and this judgment seems harsh one need only to read the tales of the doings of the gods and goddesses, or see their portrayal in relief and statue, or even be aware of the symbols carried in the religious processions or the character of the deeds and the utterances of the people in these processions.

Throughout the Old and the New Testaments God is pictured in his holiness and righteousness. The effect of this on the Israelite was to make him deeply conscious of his shortcomings and his errors. He was smitten with the thought of his sin, and cried out in anguish of heart to the merciful judge. And exactly this fact is one so completely missing among the Greeks. Though we will return to this matter later, it is adduced here as evidence for the wide difference of view between the Greek and the Hebrew. The Israelite knew a holy God, and His commands to holiness. Therefore he became contrite of heart and confessed himself a sinner. All this is very different from Greek religion. Because the Greek put beauty first the fearful condemnation of self as a transgressor of inexorable moral demands is lacking. The idea of sin does not at all pervade Greek literature as it does that of the Christian scriptures.

Though the Greek made too much of beauty at the expense of goodness one cannot but admire him for his fine sense of what constituted the beautiful. Compared with the Oriental he shows himself a different kind of individual. The Greek worshipped his god in that which is limited and definitely confined. The Oriental lost himself in that which is colossal, in the massive, that which is vast and has tremendous expanse. But the Greek built comparatively small temples, in which there was beauty of line and symmetry of form. In those temples he placed the images of his gods. But again what a difference. The Oriental conceives his god in a grotesque form. The Hindu sees him with many arms, the Egyptian portrays him as a cow, or the head of a jackel. The Chinese sees him with a fearfully distorted visage. But the Greek represents his god as a human being with a perfect physique and a benign human face. His highest concept of the beautiful expressed itself in the fine workmanship of man himself.

Because the Greek lacked the consciousness of a holy God who abhorred all evil, and therefore also lacked the sense of sin, he worshipped with a joyousness of spirit. The procession in honor of the god was not one of deep solemnity, but that of a joyous crowd. It was a festive occasion, something of an outing in which colorful pomp, gorgeous display and a generous levity of spirit revealed themselves. The Greek was not cast down in soul, crying out because of his sins "O wretched man that I am," or "God, be merciful to me, a sinner." The latter characterizes Christian thought and feeling. But the Greek trod the earth with a nimble step. The awfulness of sin in the sight of a holy God never perturbed his soul. Instead of the thought of worthlessness, and contamination of sin overwhelming his heart, his worship rested upon a sense of pride. He was making a contribution to his god, and was quite important and necessary for the god himself.

A very important element in the religious life of the Greeks was the image of the god. The reaction of Paul to this image worship was exceedingly strong. It fired his spirit with hostility to see these images on every hand.[10] It moved him to the depths of his being. Everywhere in his letters there are references to the idols and the vanity of image-worship. As a real Jew his reaction to these images was most vehement. Why?

The Greek made his image of God in the likeness of man. He felt that the most noble thing he could think of as a means of representing the divinity was man himself. Man was the nearest approach to the divine, and therefore an idealized human form was the most adequate means of conveying his thought of the god. And through the idealzed man there was wrought a certain elevation of spirit. The masterpieces, such as the Zeus of Pheidias at Olympia, glistening in gold and ivory, forty-feet high as he sat in the temple, made a profound impression on the minds of men. Dio Chrysostom, describes it thus: "Our Zeus is peaceful and kindly to all as becomes a ruler watching over a Greece without strife, and united. — Gentle and dignified in form, raised above all pain, giver of life and all its needs, and all good things, father and saviour and guardian of all men. — If a man were in sore anguish of heart, having encountered many mischances and sorrows in life, so that he could not partake of sleep; if he came into the

---

10. Cf. Acts 17.

presence of this image, he would forget all sadness and se-
verity of human life." [11]   But withal the idea also conveyed
itself through the statue as well as the mythological tales, that
the god was little above man.   The good side of that was its
counteraction of the extremely magical, wonderworking element as found in other religions.   But what an effect other
works of art must have had when the artist portrayed the gods
as descending to human level.   And even in the case of the
masterpieces the mind of the worshiper was stocked with the
tales of Homer and the poets about the escapades and the
amours of these very gods.   Again these gods were painted on
the vases which were in daily use or served as ornaments.   Or
the wall-paintings, as at Pompeii, pictured these very scenes
of the amours of the gods.   Is it any wonder that these very
images and paintings of the gods dragged down to low levels
of morality instead of having an uplifting and ennobling effect?   The poet Terence says that a young man who looked at
one of the paintings remarked "If Jupiter did it, why should
not I?"   Both Greece and Rome suffered the same weakness
in their religion.   In neither case, as in Christianity, was religion, the worship of the gods, bound up most intimately and
inseparably with genuine morality.   Both the Old and the
New Testament teach the perfect holiness of God not only,
but enjoin it upon men.   "Be ye holy, as I am holy." [12]

If the question is asked why these supposedly intellectual
Greeks made these images of the gods the answer is that it
was a concession to the weakness of men in comprehending the
gods properly.   This at least is the explanation of the Platon-
ist Maximus Tyrius of the second century, A. D.   "God is
the Father and Creator of the things that are, older than the
sun, older than the heaven, master of time and eternity and
of all changing nature.   To Him law cannot give a name, nor
can voice describe Him, nor eye behold Him.   It is because
we are not able to apprehend His being that we lean upon

11. Dio Chrysostom Or. XII, 51.
12. *Leviticus* 11:44; 19:2.

words, and names, and animal forms, and representations of gold and ivory and silver, and plants and rivers, and mountain-tops and groves. Craving for knowledge of Him, in our weakness we give to earthly things the name of good and beautiful from His nature. It is like the case of lovers to whose sight representations of their beloved give most pleasure." [13]

In how far were the two, the god and the image, identified? Among the more intellectual the deity and the image were not identified. At least in many writers the god-concept rises above the mere local representation. But the masses and the popular mind made no such distinction. The image was the divinity. It is against that view that Paul reacts.[14] But among the leaders of the Stoics there was an insight into the meaninglessness of the images. So Seneca, a contemporary of Paul, writes: "Thou shalt not form him of silver and gold; a true likeness of God cannot be moulded of this material."[15] He argues that any material representation of the god is unworthy.

Against this pagan representation of God St. Paul especially set himself like flint. Over against the many gods he placed the One God, and Jesus Christ. Over against the images he placed the invisible one in the heavens. And contrary to their laxity in morals St. Paul preached the high demands of a rigorous morality in accord with the will of the One God of heaven and earth.

This belief in one God, in other words, in a true monotheism, had very specific consequences in the field of worship. It led to a positive and emphatic exclusiveness which clashed violently with the views of the pagan world. In a polytheistic world the many gods all claimed worship, and the ancient pagan had no objection not only to serving more than one, but even felt obligated. They all must receive their due. And he had no inherent objection to the addition of one or more

13. Max. Tyrius VIII, 10.
14. Cf. Acts 17.
15. Ep. Mor. XXXI, 11.

gods, to whom he would also render worship. Hence he did not object to the introduction of this new God-Man Jesus, as such. The trouble arose from the fact that the followers of Jesus would not reciprocate. Instead of their adding Him to the recognized list of divinities, these Christians demanded sole allegiance to Him. All others were vain idols, and it was the gravest of sins to worship any other creature as God. All pagan beliefs were willing to add other divinities, but these Christians alone refused addition and recognition of all other divinities. This Christ alone is Lord, God, and none else.

In that attitude, which the Roman world regarded as plain stubbornness, lay the fundamental cause of the persecution of the early Church. On the part of the Christians the refusal to acknowledge the Roman divinities and to swear by the genius of the Emperor and to call him lord was motivated by strictly religious considerations. But the attitude of the Roman government was one of political motivation. The Emperor was head of the state which was supreme also in religious matters. Therefore the refusal on the part of the Christians to swear by his genius was high treason, and could not be tolerated. A bit of interesting evidence is given by E. M. Pickman. He points out that though Manichaeism and Mithraism held to the same kind of philosophy, the former only was persecuted by Diocletian. For the Mithraist was willing to serve in the army, take his oath by the genius of the Emperor, and thus was regarded as a loyal citizen. The Manichaean shrank from acts of violence and would not serve in the army. Both he and the Christian were therefore held to be disloyal to the empire, and the Christians had to be exterminated.[16]

16. Cf. Pickman, E. M. *The Mind of Latin Christendom,* p. 16.

CHAPTER X

The Nature of Man[1]

THUS FAR the inquiry has been engaged in investigating various angles of the view of God generally held by the ancients and those of Christianity. We now pass on to the view of man. And exactly as in the case of the views about God it was seen that the fundamental concepts were of great significance, so too here. But apparently this phase of the relation between the pagan and the Christian views has not drawn the attention, certainly has not received it, as has the view of God. The God concept is indeed most fundamental, and accordingly received ample attention in the early church. But this is no less a real fundamental, and the answer given as to the real nature of man carries with it direct consequences for one's own life, as to how he ought to live, as well as how he ought to look at and conduct himself toward his fellow man. The early Church not only, but the Church down the ages has not been aware of the significance of the question. The literature of the Church is filled with the condemnation of the inadequate and erroneous views of paganism about God and his relation to the world. But one looks in vain for a similar appraisal of man. There are statements which disapprove or condemn the extremes to which the Greek view has led, but not of the basic position itself. Thus you will find condemnations of the intellectualism of the Greeks, while at the same time accepting the basic view. For it would appear that there is something wrong when on the one hand intellectualism is attacked and condemned, while one at the same time holds to the so-called primacy of the intellect, and therefore constantly

1. I regret that the valuable contributions on this point of Dooyeweerd and Vollenhoven of the Free University of Amsterdam were not available at the time the material in this chapter was written.

describe man as a rational being. If man is essentially a rational being then he who uses that intellect and that to the full is the highest and noblest example of man. And then no condemnation is in order. But much of the otherwise excellent Christian literature is replete with precisely the view that man is essentially a rational being. I shall take the example of two of the greatest personages in the history of the Church. Neither St. Augustine nor Calvin has risen entirely above the pagan conception, and through their writings have influenced all succeeding generations. A number of statements from St. Augustine are hereby given without comment. Some of them are very explicit, so much so in fact, that one could readily imagine himself reading a pagan author. "For man, as the ancients have defined him, is a rational, mortal animal;" Vol. III p. 109; "He made man also after his own image and likeness, in the mind: for in that is the image of God." Vol. III p. 369; "The Lord Jesus knew whereby the soul of man, that is, the rational mind, made after the image of God, could be satisfied." Vol. VI. p. 540; "in the image of God. Where is the image of God? In the mind, in the intellect." Vol. VII p. 20; "And in what was he made after God's image? In the intellect, in the mind, in the inner man; in that he understands truth, distinguishes between right and wrong, knows by whom he is made, is able to understand his Creator, to praise his Creator." Vol. VII p. 508; "We perceive then that we have a certain part, in which is the image of God; viz. the mind and reason." Vol. VIII p. 140; "But furthermore, dearly beloved, we ought to remember, that after the image of God we have been made, and that not in any other part than in the understanding itself." Vol. VIII p. 210; "For I do not travel very far for examples, when I mean to give thee some similitude to thy God from thy own mind; because surely not in the body, but in that same mind, was man made after the image of God." Vol. VII p. 155. On the supremacy of the mind: "For since man is most properly understood to be made in God's image, no doubt it is that part of him by which he rises above those lower parts he has in common with the beasts, which brings him nearer to the supreme." Vol. I. p. 438; "For if we rightly call the mind the chief thing in man, that is, as it were, the head of the human substance, although the man himself together with the mind is man." Vol. III p. 102; "It is not then the soul, but that which is chief in the soul, that is called mind." Vol. III p. 205; "Therefore, as the soul is superior to the body, so in the soul itself the reason is superior by the law of nature to the other parts which are found also in the beasts; and in reason itself, which is partly contemplation and partly action, contemplation is unquestionably the superior part." Vol. IV p. 283; "For we rightly understand that as being the head which has the preeminence in the soul; and by which it is evident that the other parts of man are ruled and governed." Vol. VI. p. 47; "I on my side certainly admit, and you on your part say the same, that that is properly called spirit by which we reason and understand." Vol. V. p. 369; "in which all things are so arranged, that that which is chief and preeminent in man rules without resistance over the other elements, which are common to us with the beasts; and that very element which is preeminent in man, i. e. mind and reason, is brought under subjection to something better still, which is the truth itself, the only begotten Son of God." Vol. VI p. 5 cf. Vol. III p. 331; Vol. II p. 527; Vol. IV p. 47; Vol. IV p. 96.

Calvin speaks in the same vein as St. Augustine. "Now the mind holds the highest rank in the human constitution, is the seat of reason, presides over the will, and restrains sinful desires." Ephesians p. 289; "Be renewed in the spirit, or, be renewed within or completely — beginning with the mind, which appears to be the part most free from all taint of sin." idem p. 296;" But I have no doubt, Paul's intention was, to guard us against allowing Satan to take possession of our minds and, by keeping in his hands this citadel, to do whatever he pleases." Idem p. 299; "The first (pneuma) is that we have like views; the second (psyche) that we be united in heart. For when these two terms are connected together spirit denotes the understanding, while soul denotes the will." Phil. p. 46; "Hence, when we find mention made here of the term spirit, let us understand it as denoting reason or intelligence, as on the other hand by the term soul, is meant the will and all the affections." Phil. p. 105; "Now see what kind of a renovation is required from us; It is not that of the flesh only, or of the inferior part of the soul; but of the mind, which is the most excellent part of us, and to which philosophers ascribe the supremacy, for they call it 'hegemonikon' the leading power, and reason is imagined to be a most wise queen. But Paul pulls her down from her throne, and so reduces her to nothing by teaching us that we must be renewed in mind." Rom. p. 454; "For what is more noble than man's reason, in which man excels other animals." I Cor. p. 82; "Now though the heart more frequently denotes the will or the seat of the affections, yet here it is put for the understanding." Harm. Vol. II p. 339 on Mk. 6:52; "The heart is sometimes in Scripture put for the seat of the affections; but here, as in many other passages, it denotes what is called the intellectual part of the soul." John Vol. II p. 43, on John 12:40. On John 13:21 'he was troubled in spirit' "Spirit here denotes the understanding or the soul." John Vol. II p. 67; "Fourthly he showeth that nothing is more absurd than to draw any portraiture of God, seeing that the mind of man is his true image," Acts Vol. II p. 133; "For man has not only been ensnared by the inferior appetites, but abominable impiety has seized the very citadel of his mind, and pride has penetrated into the inner-most recesses of his heart. Whence it follows that that part, which principally displays the excellence and dignity of the soul, is not only wounded, but so corrupted, that it requires not merely to be healed but to receive a new nature." Inst. p. 230, 231; The reader will have noticed the tendency of Calvin to equivalate spirit (pneuma) and even heart with the mind, exactly as St. Augustine did. Both speak very much like Philo Judaeus.

Apparently men have thought that on this matter of the essential nature of man the pagan view of Greece and Rome could be trusted, accepted and propagated. But can it? Is there an indentity of view or a real difference? And if the latter what are the consequences? To this question we now set ourselves.

The conception of man as contained in the New Testament naturally follows the historical line of its Israelite antecedents. Christianity bases its view on the Old Testament, and especially on the Genesis account of man's creation. Man is declared to be made after the image of God. And Christian teaching holds this to be true of both soul and body. It is because the body is viewed in that light that genuine Christianity does not reveal a false asceticism such as manifested itself in Pythagoreanism, Platonism, and also in Stoicism. Since the point is of great importance a fuller discussion of it will be taken up later under the heading Soul and Body.

The specific references in the New Testament are found in I Cor. 11:7 and James 3:9. Man is made in the image of God. The point to be emphasized is that in saying that, Christian teaching does not mean to express the essential oneness with God. Man is made after the pattern of the Godhead, but he is not divine and does not share in divinity. There remains an essential difference between God and man, between Creator and creature.

But in Greek thought the essential oneness of God and man is taught. There is a unity by which man is not distinct from divinity. The truly divine in man is his intellect. In tracing the history of the idea it is not necessary to go beyond Heracleitus. With him the term "logos" arises and persists through the whole course of Greek philosophy and Roman Stoicism. The word is descriptive of the highest and ultimate substance, and emphasizes reason and rationality. Anaxagoras substitutes the word nous, and in Plato and Aristotle this word often expresses the idea. The substance, however, is the same. Plato taught that the soul is of divine origin and nature, and that it is the same as the soul of the world. Nothing need be said of Aristotle because he did not believe in the soul as an entity. Especially among the Stoics the view of the divinity of man is very pronounced. The clew goes back to Heracleitus, who taught that the primary substance was fire and that Logos was indentical with it. This Logos permeates all things. Hence too, man has a share in it, really possesses a part of it. Their view is not that man is inspired and enlightened by the Logos. That too, but much more. Man is a portion of its very substance. That being the case, one can understand their emphasis on immanence. The destiny of the soul, therefore, is again to be assimilated to the divine principle whence it came. That view of the divinity of the soul is the source of their disdain of the body. The glorious hope is once again to be free from its bondage, to live apart from the body and the world.

According to Stoicism man is a fragment of the divine. A few examples will suffice. Seneca wrote, "Reason is nothing else than a part of the divine spirit immersed in the human body."[2] Again he says, "Between good men and the gods a friendship exists, virtue being the bond of amity. Friendship do I say? Nay more, it is a clear relationship and likeness, since the good man differs from God only in time; he is his pupil and imitator, his true offspring."[3] In like vein Epictetus says, "But if our souls are so bound up with God and joined together with him, as being parts of his being, does not God perceive their every motion as being a motion of that which is his own and of one body with himself?"[4]

The emperor Aurelius says, "And thou hast forgotten too that every man's intelligence is a god and an efflux of the deity."[5] "and he does live with the gods who constantly shows to them that his own soul is satisfied with that which is assigned to him, and that it does all that the demon wished, which Zeus hath given to every man for his guardian and guide, a portion of himself. And this is every man's understanding and reason."[6] The quotations have been numerous in this case because they indicate not only the matter in hand, but also make evident the intellectualism pervading their

---

2. Ep. 66, 12; cf. 92, 1.
3. De Prov. I, 5.
4. Disc. I, X, IV, 6; cf. I, XVII, 27; II, VIII 11-12; Cicero: Rep. VI, 24; De Leg. I, VII, 23; I, XXII, 59; Tusc. Disp. I, 26, 65; Horace's Satires II, 2, 77-79; Virgil Aeneid VI, 724-732.
5. Med. XII, 26.
6. Med. V, 27.

teaching. The significant point is that in much of modern thought there is a return to, or rather a reiteration of pagan thought. The vaunted divinity of man, and the "divine spark" in every individual is nothing but the teaching of the ancient pagans, and it is completely divergent from Christian thought as expressed in the Scripture.

According to the ancients then there is identity of substance between God and man. And again when one asks what is the real nature of that substance the answer given is that it is nous, intelligence. Therefore the essential nature of man too is to be found in the intellect. Man's soul is divine, and the real soul is the intellect. Aristotle says, "Man is the only animal that stands upright and this is because his nature and essence is divine. Now the business of that which is most divine is to think and to be intelligent."[7] Though the liberals have not hestitated to agree with the ancients on both scores, orthodox Christianity has vehemently denied the divinity of the soul but apparently has accepted the view that man is essentially intellect. The teaching of the ancients on the faculties of the soul, together with the elevation of the intellect to the place of supremacy has had marked influence.

When one looks carefully at Greek thought it appears to some to reveal agreement with Christianity. The division of the soul into three parts as developed especially in Plato's Republic is most significant though the same thought occurs in other dialogues.[8] In the body these parts are very definitely localized. First is the intellect which resides in the head; below that is the spirited part resident in the chest and expressing itself in courage, anger; still lower is the purely appetitive part. The ideal relation between these parts is that the mind should rule, and that "spirit" and "appetite" should be servants willing to carry out the dictates of the mind. But appetite and spirit are of a rebellious nature and frequently rise up against "reason" and overthrow its behests. To keep this from happening the gods fashioned man's body in a most curious and wise manner. Because the appetites are so

---

7. Parts of Animals 686a27-29.
8. Timaeus, Symposuim, Phaedrus.

strong and frequently win over the spirited part, man has been so fashioned as to keep these rebellious parts from rushing headlong on the citadel of reason. Plato half seriously gives that as the reason for man's having a small neck. For the urges of his lower nature rise up and rush to overthrow reason. The gods foresaw this and therefore in their wisdom so made man that these urges are caught in a jam, with the result that they can not overthrow reason so readily. Plato would picture it as a kind of bottle-neck in the stream of psychic traffic. Reason in its clarity should guide the individual, and to prevent the other two from usurping the place of reason the passage to the mind has been made narrow intentionally. We smile and say that the thought is very ingenious. At another time Plato uses the beautiful figure of the charioteer and his steeds.[9] The mind then is the charioteer, and the other parts of the soul are the steeds. The thought is the same. In both cases it is mind, intellect that is supreme and is required to give direction. Plato plays with this idea of the supremacy of reason in various ways. That too is the explanation of man's upright position. The nobility of his intellect, akin to that of the gods, is manifest in that the gods have placed it in that part of man nearest to the abode of the gods. Man, as it were, hangs from above, where there is intelligence.[10] And because his intellect is so precious the gods have taken precautions to protect it. Therefore they incased it in a strong skull, and again covered it with soft hair which serves as protection.

This all amuses in a measure. But Plato most seriously taught the supremacy of the mind. That his thought is serious is also evident from what he says about immortality. Really, the mind alone is immortal. Of these three parts of the soul only one, the mind survives after death. When the mind is incarnated or as Plato would say, incarcerated, spirited and appetitive parts are linked to it only so long as it resides in the body.

9. Phaedrus 247.
10. Timaeus 90a.

Looked at from a slightly different point of view Plato and the Stoics later see man as composed of mind, soul, and body. Now there are those who think that the New Testament teaches the same thing. But these very writers seem to be unaware of a real difference. The only difference, they maintain, is that spirit (pneuma) is substituted for "mind." But that is exactly the point. It is not a mere substitution of another word; for the content of the two is different and therefore the triad of Christian thought is not that of Plato, as Dean Inge thinks.[11]

The only passages in which it seems that man has a tripartite nature are I Cor. 15:44-45, Heb. 4:12, and I Thess. 5:23. It is especially the last passage which is quoted as evidence of this view. On various occasions Paul speaks of spirit and soul. The first conclusion would therefore be that these two have a constant difference of meaning. But that is not the case. At times the two are used interchangeably. And in the passage under consideration the terms are used more as a rhetorical device than as a strictly logical distinction. Paul is zealous to have the whole man dedicated to God, and therefore uses various words to give expression to his desire. The Pauline teaching is not that of a real difference between spirit and soul in the sense that they are two entities, but rather this that the soul looked at from different angles is both spirit and soul.

The difference is this. In the foregoing it was indicated that the highest term in which the New Testament writers conceive of God is Pneuma, spirit. Nowhere does the Scripture say that God is nous, intelligence. In the thought of Paul the term pneuma occupies a unique place. In all the literature before him there is no such prominence given to the term.[12] The thought of Paul seems to be this. The noblest, deepest, and highest in man is pneuma. It is that which is

---

11. Inge, W. R.: Platonic Tradition in English Religious Thought pp. 12-14.
12. Burton, E.: Spirit, Soul, and Flesh p. 187.

the point of contact between God and man. It is the religious side of man, his religious nature. Through regeneration man receives the Pneuma of God, and through His operation in the individual, man is made pneuma, and is called by Paul a pneumatic being. Thereby he expresses the relation of the believer to God and at the same time gives an indication of his true nature. Deep down the believer is a spiritual being. born of the Father of spirits, and not only a psychical one.

Every man is psyche or soul, but only the Christian has pneuma. The soul is that through which the spirit of man expresses itself. It is that which gives individuality, is that which is the seat of the personal impressions. It stands, in a sense, midway between the spirit and the body, and is the mediating element between the two. It forms the means of contact between the material and the spiritual side of man.

The pneuma then is that which refers to the religious experiences and capacities of the soul. The real man in the Christian is therefore the pneumatic one. How different from Plato, and Greek thought generally! To indicate what is highest in man the Greeks spoke of the mind (nous). But Paul constantly emphasizes that which is above mind, i. e. pneuma which includes more than intelligence. When a man has pneuma he is influenced by it in mind, feeling, will.

The term, therefore, is broader and richer than the nous of the Greeks. By putting the emphasis there, Paul has at the same time pointed out the contrast between Greek and Christian thinking. Just because the Greek maintained that the highest in man was mind, he was bound to overemphasize mind and fall into intellectualism. The first clear statement of this intellectualism is found in the Socratic maxim that knowledge is virtue. Plato affirms it when he says, "the virtue of intelligence seems to be something more divine and to unite men with gods and with the life of the gods."[13] It led Aristotle to say that reason" seems to exercise rule and authority by natural right and to have a conception of things

13. Rep. 518d-e.

noble and divine, because it is either itself divine or is rela-
tively the most divine part of our being. . . If then the reason is divine in comparison with the rest of human nature,
the life which accords with reason will be divine in comparison with human life in general. . . It would seem too that
the reason is the true self of a man-if a man's true self is the
highest or best in him.,"[14] and that the life of the gods is
"thinking upon thought."[15]

   At the beginning it was said that the two streams of pagan
and Christian thought have mingled together to make modern
civilization. With the Revival of Learning the Greek spirit
emptied itself into the civilization of Western Europe. That
spirit expressed itself as having a great love of knowledge.
And since the Renaissance that is often regarded as its greatest contribution. Can it be that the West has taken over the
Greek emphasis on the intellect at the expense of a genuine
Christian outlook? Until very recently men put all their confidence in the scientific method and the advance of science.
Does not the glorification of the intellect express itself in that
hope? When one compares the cardinal virtues of the Greeks
with those of Christianity is there not a vast difference? The
Greeks seek wisdom, intellectual comprehension and insight.
Christian thought transfers you to the realm of love. But
more of this later.

----
14. Nic. Ethics 1177b.
15. Meta. 1074b34.

CHAPTER XI

The Pre-existence of the Soul

WE MUST pause for a few moments to consider a question which is largely of academic significance. For whether one answers that the soul was or was not existent prior to its entrance in the body is not of any specific practical concern. Unless, to be sure, one uses that doctrine to explain a portion of the phenomena of life as it is lived by men in time. And that has been the use of the doctrine, as will be seen in a few moments.

Does the soul exist apart from and antecedent to the body? What is the answer of Christian and of Greek thought? That the soul can and does exist apart from and independent of the body Christianity definitely affirms. But it generally restricts this belief to the existence after death. There is only one passage in the New Testament that has any direct bearing on this question. In John 9:2 the doctrine seems to be definitely implied. What else can the text mean when the question is whether this man sinned so that he was born blind? It seems that the passage is rarely understood in that light, and yet the implication seems entirely clear that the man's present condition is the result either of his own or his parent's doing. And if his own, then clearly the condition of his being blind must be the reward or punishment for conduct in a previous existence. That still leaves the question open as to the nature of that existence. Does it refer to a state of the soul apart from a body, or is the reference to a former incarnation? Have we here a slight evidence of the penetration of Pythagorean and Platonic conceptions into Palestinian territory? For surely Plato taught both the preexistence of the soul and the reincarnation.[1] Although various passages[2] in Scripture are adduced as evidence of the teaching of preexistence this is done without sufficient ground.

Whence then did the view originate? Porbably it came ultimately from Pythagorean or Platonic sources, but more directly from Jewish writings which were influenced by the Greek tradition. In the Wisdom of Solomon we read, "For I was a child of parts, and a good soul fell to my lot; nay, rather, being good, I came into a body undefiled."[3] And again we read, "Every soul was created eternally before the foundation of the world."[4] The doctrine was well known to Jewish writers, but is originally Greek.

This Greek view has influenced many in the Church during the ages. Origen believed it.[5] Jerome at one time held to it. Augustine did not deny it, and the question was not officially decided until the time of Gregory the Great. Later it was again championed by the Cambridge Platonists who followed the Neo-Platonic speculations of earlier ages.

1. Cf. Phaedrus, Phaedo, Republic, Timaeus.
2. Cf. Jer. 1:5; Ps. 139:16; Eph. 1:4.
3. Wisdom of Solomon 8:19-20.
4. Secrets of Enoch 23:5.
5. Contra Celsum VII, 50.

CHAPTER XII

Soul and Body

IT HAS already been indicated that there was much in Greek thought which denied a thorough-going materialism as to the nature of man. Many recognized that he had a physical and a pyschical self. In that respect there is identity between the two main streams of thought under consideration. But the similarity ceases when one investigates not the relation between these two as to their functioning (that will not be discussed) but the relative value of soul and body, and the consequent attitude toward the body. For the attitude which regards the body as itself evil, as a hindrance to the soul, as a prison in which the soul is kept, and which is the cause of its going astray will lead to asceticism. The question must therefore be faced whether on this fundamental pagan and Christian thought are the same.

It can safely be said that the Greeks as a people were far from ascetic. One of their outstanding characteristics was their intense humanism. The Greek generally felt very well at home in the world. Fact is that he felt too well at home. He really enjoyed living, although not quite so buoyantly as he is sometimes pictured, as though he was as carefree as a little child. But in the main he loved life. Because he so loved it he had no strong urge toward ascetic movements, which give expression to the desire to get away from life and out of the present world. Ascetic tendencies and movements are generally missing from the Greek attitude toward life. Such movements as one finds are not truly Greek, and do not spring from Greek but Oriental soil. Whatever monastic life is found in early Christianity had its origins in Egypt where the great monasteries of Serapis existed long before the Christian era.

The Greek as a rule did not despise the body. His interest in athletic contests and his admiration of a beautiful body is sufficient evidence. Every kind of activity was undertaken and practised to develop strong, agile, beautiful bodies. Their opposition to certain forms of work was precisely because in the long run they affected the form, strength, and health of the body. Ascetic tendencies were foreign to the Greek soul, and were generally regarded as in contrast with the normal way of living. The opposition was so strong that asceticism was regarded as something of a paradox, and almost as heresy. For they were "extremes" and that the Greek with his temperance, balance, and moderation could not endure.

In much of Greek literature we do find that the body is regarded as evil in itself and as a hindrance to the soul. The outstanding instance, of course, is Plato. Before giving some references to specific utterances on this point the contrast between Greek and Hebrew must again be noticed. Both had an attitude expressive of criticism of the body, but the fault found is quite different. The Greek quarreled with the body because he was an intellectual being. It was noted above that the Greek saw in the mind, the intellect, the real essence of man. But the body stood in the way of the mind. It demanded too much time to be fed and clothed, became ill and weak so that thought-activity could not be carried on, and its desires drew away from the contemplation of the good, the true, and the beautiful.[1] The body, its care and desires, prevent and hinder thinking, or rather right thinking. At best the Greek regarded man's body as that which he has in common with the brutes. So Epictetus later expresses it.[2] Only his reason and intelligence he has in common with

---

1. Cf. Plato's Phaedo.
2. Dis. I, 111, 1.

the gods. The Greek mystic scorned the body because it limited or thwarted the intellectual contemplation of the divine.

But the Hebrew looked at the body from another angle. Because he did not glorify the intellect as the supreme element in man, and as a consequence did not revel in intellectual, critical acumen, but had a stern moral sense his grievance against the body was not that it hindered or prevented right thinking, but right living, or doing. In other words his reaction was in the moral sphere. The body was the means of keeping from noble living. It stood in the way of morality, not of intellectuality. And worse than that it led men on to terrible vices. St. Paul following in the Hebrew tradition takes this position.

Having made the qualification mentioned above it is time to mention some specific ascetic tendencies in Greek history. The first important movements are Orphism and Pythagoreanism which began already in the sixth century. In them we find the first real emphasis on the duality of man. In their teaching the soul was regarded as divine, but imprisoned in the body. The way of life was therefore to get away from the body through an ascetic ordering of life itself. The body is a "tomb" and man must be released from it.

In Plato there is a strain of Pythagorean influence, and his writings gave a mighty stimulus to the idea that the body is a hindrance to the highest activities of the soul. According to Homer the soul is only the shadowy image of the body but Plato reverses this traditional order. The body now becomes only an image of the soul.[3] Pure and real happiness can be had only when the soul is freed from the body. The classic expression of this idea is in the Phaedo. There the body is regarded as a "prison house" to the soul and the ideal is to get as far away from it as possible. This position led to the extreme mysticism of Neo-platonism; and naturally

---

3. Laws 959.

it had a very definite influence on the attitude toward the question of the resurrection of the body.

Among the very many traits of the Hellenistic Age is also this one of an increased Mysticism. It seems, looking back over the ages, now to be readily explained. The world, life externally had not given the desired results. And again the activity of the mind in thought had not brought about inward peace and happiness. The result would seem natural. There was a dual turning, first away from the external world as the source of inspiration and hope, and secondly away from thought as offering the solution to the troubles of life. The turning was toward inwardness, but that not to the intellect, but to the emotions, to feeling. Consequently there arose the consciousness of a sharp division between soul and body. There arose an intense longing for release from the finite world and its limitations; a burning desire to be freed from the weight of the body. Men wanted to arrive at the world of rapture and ecstacy. It can be put down as a mark of the Graeco-Roman world that men wanted a deliverance from the body and the world. In that sense there was longing for salvation. To be sure, it was largely negative. The gospel which was to come urges men not only to flee from the world but gives the positive command to conquer the world; not to get out of the body but to subject all its members to Christ and his will. Later Jewish thought has been influenced toward taking the Greek attitude toward the body. In the Book of Wisdom we read, "This corruptible body weighs down the soul and the earthly tabernacle weighs heavy upon the care-encumbered mind."[4] Thus Philo, a contemporary of Paul, often speaks of the body in the terms of the Orphics and Neo-Pythagoreans as the "prison house of the soul"[5] although in one passage the body is "a sacred temple of the rational soul." In this respect Philo is at one with the Stoics who regarded

---

4. Wisdom of Solomon 9:15.
5. De Opifici Mundi 137; De Migratione Abraham 9; Leg. Allegoriarum III, 41ff; idem III 47.

the body as a prison-house. Seneca especially speaks in this vein and life becomes a long punishment.[6] "The frail body is to be regarded as necessary rather than important."[7] Again he says, "I regard this body as nothing but a chain which manacles my freedom."[8]

The teaching of the New Testament must now be considered. There are a number of passages which deal with the subject, among which the following are important.[9] In all these passages we find an idea which gives rise to the view that Christianity in Paul regards the body as essentially evil. And it must be admitted that when these passages alone are read there is ground for such an interpretation. Thus Gilbert writes: "with Greek philosophy in general he (Paul) thinks of the body as the prison of the spirit. Rom. 8:23; II Cor. 5:4."[10] The same kind of interpretation is given by Scott when he writes: "The flesh is no mere weakness of man's nature, exposing him to the assaults of evil, but is itself the positive source of evil. Rom. 7:18; 8:8."[11]

The most compelling reply to such interpretations is not found in quoting individual texts which teach the contrary, but rather by putting certain indisputable teachings of Christianity and Paul over against it. We have already touched on one. If the body is essentially evil how can one believe the resurrection of the body? Yet, Paul clearly teaches such a resurrection. But the essential sinfulness of the body would necessarily preclude any such resurrection. And again, how is the doctrine of Incarnation to be squared with such a belief? Christ in the Incarnation assumes the human body, and is like unto us in all things save sin. How is this possible, if having a body is from the very nature of the case having

6. Ep. 120 14; 65, 16; Ad Polyb. 9, 6; Ad Marc. 22, 2; idem 24, 5.
7. Ep. 23, 6.
8. Ep. 65, 21.
9. Rom. 7:14ff; 7:24; 8:23; I Cor. 6:15; II Cor. 5:4; Gal. 5:17; Col. 3:5.
10. Greek Thought in the New Testament, p. 86.
11. The Gospel and Its Tributaries, p. 146.

something sinful? Two of the fundamentals of Christian thought, the Incarnation and the Resurrection, could not be maintained on the premise that the body is essentially evil.

Further, there are specific passages which militate against and deny such an interpretation of the passages listed above.[12] It is true that "sarx" and "soma" are nearly synonymous in one long passage.[13] But on the other hand Paul urges "to cleanse ourselves from all defilement of flesh and spirit."[14] And positively, the believers are members of Christ.[15]

In conclusion it may be said that instead of teaching an essential evil of the body Scripture declares that there are two spheres, the natural and the spiritual. These two are not related as evil and good, but as the lower and the higher.[16] The passages[17] are the expression of this idea. The body is looked at from the point of view of the power of sin and its fearful results.

The primitive Church met on every hand this Greek conception of the body as being evil for it was accepted by most philosophies. But the Church stood on the basis of the Old Testament, declaring that God was the creator of the world of matter as well as of the world of spirit. This emphasis and reiteration is found frequently in the apologists, and is finally taken up in the official creed in the words, "I believe in God the Father, Creator of heaven and earth." For that fundamental misconception of the Greek mind was at the bottom of the opposition to the belief in the Incarnation and the Resurrection both.

---

12. I Cor. 6:13; 6:19.
13. Rom. 7:14-25.
14. II Cor. 7:1.
15. I Cor. 6:15; I Cor. 12; Rom. 12.
16. John 3:6.
17. Rom. 7:18; 7:24; 8:8.

CHAPTER XIII

Man's Present State

In a Preceding chapter it was pointed out that in Greek thought man was regarded as essentially divine. To all however it was apparent that man did not live on the high level of true divinity. What then was their conception of his present state? The contrast on this point between the two systems of thought is very pronounced. It is put effectively in the words of Mathew Arnold: "As one passes and repasses from Hellenism to Hebraism, from Plato to St. Paul, one feels inclined to rub one's eyes and ask oneself whether man is indeed a gentle and simple being, showing the traces of a noble and divine nature, or an unhappy chained captive, laboring with groanings that cannot be uttered to free himself from the body of this death."[1] In the Old Testament man's state is described as "desperately wicked" and this is carried on into the New Testament. But the Greek did not feel that man is a fearfully sinful being. For him the vast majority of mankind possessed a mediocre moral character. Man was neither exceptionally good nor bad. What characterized him was weakness and limitation.

In so far as he was bad this was due to lack of insight and failure to comprehend truly. The task was therefore to impart right knowledge so that true insight might be attained, and men would as a matter of course become good. If the Greek had recognized the desperate state of man it would have been only in the sphere of the intellect. From this source, that man is ignorant, short-sighted, intellectually obtuse, arises the dictum that the way out is through knowledge. Socrates sum-

---

1. Culture and Anarchy p. 117.

marized it in "knowledge is virtue," and "no man does evil voluntarily." If he does evil it is because he does not know any better. Impart knowledge to him and a brighter day will dawn. Correct his mistaken views and hold up before him the right ideals, and he will gladly accept them and conduct himself accordingly.

By contrast Christianity affirmed the need of a new birth. In its eyes man was desperately wicked and must be completely and radically remade. Mere additional knowledge is not able nor sufficient to bring about the needed change. Only supernatural grace and corresponding activity can accomplish the desired end. The emphasis of Christianity by which it was declared that man must become a new creature was generally unknown to the Greeks. In the eyes of the Greek human nature was so good that true insight would achieve all that was desirable for man. The cry of St. Paul in desperation "O wretched man that I am" finds no response in Greek thought. Who then can save him? Only grace from God himself. And when man becomes good, and as a result also does good, the only explanation is the operation not of man's spirit, but of the supernatural Spirit which enters man and gives wisdom, power, all excellence.

This view of the Greeks expressed itself fully in Roman Stoicism. There the root idea of their ethics is the dignity of human nature. Man is therefore exhorted to live according to nature, the nature of man and the universe. The assumption is that the nature of man is still good, and a sufficient guide, if man will but look within for light and power. All will gladly accept and follow the ideal held up before them. Seneca is optimistic: "It is easy to rouse a listener so that he will crave righteousness; for nature has laid the foundations and planted the seeds of virtue in us all."[2] The environmental factors spoil the natively good soul. The following statement sounds extremely modern: "The seeds of virtue are in-

---

2. Ep. Mor. CVIII 8.

born in our dispositions and, if they were allowed to ripen, nature's own hand would lead us on to happiness of life; as things are, however, as soon as we come into the light of day and have been acknowledged, we at once find ourselves in a world of iniquity amid a medley of wrong beliefs, so that it seems as if we drank in deception with our mother's milk; but when we leave the nursery to be with parents and later on have been handed over to the care of masters, then we become infected with deceptions so varied that truth gives place to unreality and the voice of nature to fixed prepossessions."[3]   Compare with this the Christian view that man is so sorely corrupt and perverted that only an act of God through rebirth can save him.   More will be said about this later. Suffice it here to point out that the question here dealt with is a fundamental one and the answer given bears fruit in many ways.   This view of the innocence and goodness of man originally developed by the Greeks repeatedly manifests itself in history.   And the denial of the Christian position of the wickedness of man has led to the neglect or denial of other Christian teachings.   The latter half of the nineteenth and early part of the twentieth centuries were characterized by this same confidence in and glorification of man.   There has been that same Stoic emphasis on knowledge, enlightenment as the way out.   But at the present time some of the liberals have returned at least part way to the true position which affirms the sinfulness of man.   Niebuhr has stated it well in these words: "The real crux of the issue between essential Christianity and modern culture lies at this point.   The conflict is between those who have a confidence in human virtue which human nature cannot support and those who have looked too deeply into life and their own souls to place their trust in so broken a reed."[4]

---

3. Cicero: Tusc. Disp. III, 1, 2-3.
4. Niebuhr, R.: An Interpretation of Christian Ethics p. 121 cf. Pickman, E.: The Mind of Latin Christendom, p. 78; Mercier, L.: Challenge of Humanism. p. 31.

CHAPTER XIV

The Last Things

THE QUESTIONS to be dealt with in this chapter are death, immortality, judgment, and the resurrection. Again the answers of the pagan world of antiquity stand in sharpest contrast to the teaching of the New Testament. The message of the Christian evangelists and apostles with reference to the future was startling to the ancient pagans. In many cases it was exactly the message of a blessed hope which drew many from paganism to the fold of Christianity. For Paul correctly describes the pagan world as without God and without hope. At this point one is tempted to linger on the word "hope" itself, since it occupies a preeminent place in the Christian virtues, but the matter will be discussed more fully later.

The New Testament sees in death a phenomenon closely related to sin, so close in fact that it is the result of sin. Here again the two testaments are in full agreement. But just because death is linked to sin it acquires an ethical and religious significance totally lacking in pagan thought. Paul lays down the Christian position in unequivocal langauge, "The wages of sin is death."[1]

According to the Greek view death is nothing but a natural phenomenon. How could it be linked to sin, when his views either denied sin entirely, or were so vague as to deny it practically? For them one of the most tragic and fundamental things in life remained without an adequate explanation. Death was thought of simply as one of the inevitable things; all must face it sooner or later. It is in accord with all of

---

1. Rom. 6:23; cf. Rom. 5:12.

nature that man too is born and eventually dies. It is therefore something natural and nothing more. This view remains
throughout Greek literature, and is found consistently in the
Stoics. Death is only a dissolution of soul and body and a
return of the various elements to the source from which they
sprang. Death therefore is nothing dreadful.[2] Seneca says
specifically "Death is no punishment, but the law of nature."
"Children and idiots do not fear death, why cannot reason
attain to that security which folly has achieved?"[3] And Marcus Aurelius wrote "Death like birth is a secret of nature —
a combination of the same elements, a breaking up into the
same — and not at all a thing in fact for any to be ashamed
of, for it is not out of keeping with an intellectual creature or
the reason of his constitution."[4]

Unfortunately altogether too much of modern thought has
followed the Greek tradition on this point. The great increase
in knowledge in the natural sciences and with it the emphasis
on and the clarity of the operation of secondary causes has
dimmed or completely obliterated the thought of the primary
cause in death. Sin has been forgotten or ignored. And
death is just one other of the many "natural phenomena."

But death, once having come, what of the future? We are
still faced with the query of Job, "If a man die, shall he live
again?" The questions multiply. What happens at death?
Is there a continued existence or is it annihilation? If there
is a continued existence what is its character? Is it a personal immortality? To these questions Christian faith answers emphatically "Yes."[5]

Greek literature generally is silent on this question. There
are of course passages which deal with it quite specifically,
but as a rule the question is hushed in silence. The present

2. Epict Dis. III. XIII. 14.
3. Ep. 36.
4. Med. IV. 5.
5. Cf. John 11:25ff; John 14:3; Luke 23:43; Luke 16:19-31; Matt. 5:29f;
11:21-24.

charmed and infatuated the Greek. The future was a vast unknown. What was to come in the future in no sense dominated Greek thought. He lived here and now and the hereafter was of little concern to him. The veil is drawn tightly over the future. In the masterly funeral orations, that of Pericles included, that which would seem a natural cause for consolation, the happy existence of the departed is not alluded to. The conclusion seems warranted that had there been a belief in a blessed immortality the subject would have been touched on. The cause for consolation lies in the past, in the heroic deeds, the life of the dead. The sepulchral monuments give ample evidence of this. On them the departed was portrayed as he or she had been, in full bloom and glory, in life. The Greek looked backward when death overtook his kin. The future was unknown. Pindar in some of his odes forms an exception, as does also Plato. But for most writers the future spelled non-existence, or an existence drained of reality. It was without real happiness, but also without pain.

Especially after Socrates the question was debated whether the soul continued to exist or not after death. The classic passage in Plato is in the Apology.[6] In the Hellenistic Age there appear the following views. The Peripatetics refused to speculate about the existence of a soul which their reason could neither conceive nor define. The Sceptics and the Academics either doubted the possibility of a future life, or suspended judgment on the problem. The Epicureans, of course, openly opposed any belief in immortality. A few instances of these views will prove interesting. Caesar opposed death for the Catilinarian conspirators because "Death puts a period to all human ills, and beyond the grave there is no opportunity for either anxiety or joy."[7] The elder Pliny vehemently

---

6. 40f.
7. Sallust' Catalina 51ff.

rejected the idea of a future life.[8]   The poet Catullus took an everlasting farewell at his brother's grave.   "Suns can set and rise again, but we, when our brief light is extinguished, must sleep for an eternal night."[9]   On grave inscriptions one reads "Once I had no existence; now I have none; I am not aware of it; I care not."   "We are and we were nothing: See reader, how swiftly we mortals go back from nothingness to nothingness."

The Stoics repeatedly manifest a real doubt as to the hereafter.   Seneca in what is supposed to be a consolation says "Then we also, happy souls who have been assigned to eternity, when God shall see fit to reconstruct the universe, when all things pass, we too, a little element in a great catastrophe, shall be resolved into our ancient elements.   Happy is your son, Marcia, who already knows this."[10]   Again he writes, "Why am I wasted for desire of him, who is either happy or non-existent."[11]   "Death is the one port in a stormy sea — it is either end or transition — it brings us back to where we were before birth — it must be gain or nothing."[12]   For "Death either annihilates us or strips us bare.   If we are then released, there remains the better part, after the burden has been withdrawn; if we are annihilated, nothing remains."[13]   And again he says "for the soul at death is either sent forth into a better life, destined to dwell with deity amid greater radiance and calm, or else, at least, without suffering any harm to itself, it will be mingled with nature again, and will return to the universe."[14]

Epictetus and Marcus Aurelius continue in the same strain. The former writes "It is now time for the material of which

8. Hist. Nat. VII, 55.
9. Catullus V, 4ff.
10. Ad Marciam, fine.
11. Ad. Polyb. 9:3.
12. Ep. 24; Cf. Cicero De Senetute XIX 66; Epistulae Ad Familiares VI, XXI.
13. Ep. Mor. XXIV 18; cf. LXV, 24.
14. Ep. Mor. LXXI 16.

you are constituted to be restored to those elements from which it came. And what is there terrible about that? What one of the things that make up the universe will be lost, what novel or unreasonable thing will have taken place?"[15]   And the emperor admonishes "to wait with a good grace for the end, whether it be extinction or translation."[16]

The question therefore was "to be or not to be." And the answer was one of doubt. Many thought death meant anni-hilation, extinction. Others of the Stoic creed interpreted it to be reabsorption into the primal elements of the universe. And of course, if the latter took place, that was the end of the continued existence of the individual. In either case the outlook was gloomy. It is not strange, therefore, that Paul described the pagan world as being without hope.

And if the answer to the question of continued existence was affirmative (and there were such answers) the picture is by no means attractive. The Homeric eschatology had a marvelous tenacity. The Greeks generally advanced little be-yond it. There was no lively hope for eternity because that existence in the hereafter had no appeal. In the beyond the souls of men are like vain shadows which are deprived of the organs of will and emotion. Like jibbering bats these souls flit hither and thither without plan or purpose. In a dank world, utterly bereft of charm, they continue to exist, but hope has left them.[17]   Worse still, memory and the power of recognition has left them.[18]   It is a dreary, chilly existence, deprived of the bright sunshine of the upper world, and the charms of human life. It is nothing but a pale, dim shadow of what is known in the world above. Odysseus recognized his mother's ghost but alas, not she him. "Thrice I sprang to-wards her, and was minded to embrace her; thrice she flitted from my hands as a shadow or even as a dream, and sharper

15. Disc. IV. 7. 15.
16. M. Aurelius V, 33. cf. IV, 21; VII, 32; VIII, 25; XI, 31.
17. Od. 24:1ff.
18. Od. 11:24ff; cf. Cicero Ad Familiares V, XXI, 4; VI, III, 4.

ever waxed the grief within me."[19] Compared to this life
the existence beyond was as nothing. "Speak not to me of
death, glorious Odysseus. For so I might be on earth, I
would rather be the servant of another, of a poor man who
had little substance than to be lord over all the dead."[20] Repeatedly in the orators and elsewhere the subject is introduced
with the sad words "If there be any consciousness in Hades."
To such a colorless existence, without bliss or pain, the multi-
tude was doomed. A few outstanding heroes went to a better
life, as did the arch criminals and fiends to a worse existence.

Plato was a believer in the immortality of the soul, but
hardly could one regard it as a personal immortality. For
Plato maintained that only the general, the universal is truly
eternal. That abides forever. But surely, the individual
soul is not a universal. How then can such a particular exist
forever? Plato has seemingly taken care of the difficulty by
his conception of man. It was stated above that the distinctive thing about man is "reason" which is immortal and in-
destructible. This "reason" enters the body of the infant.
But this "reason" has nothing in common with the particular
character and personality which that babe develops and manifests in the course of its life. For those personal traits and
characteristics depend on heredity and the circumstances of
life. These traits remain through life, but are not a permanent possession. At death all these particulars, these personal characteristics drop away and only the purely rational
part of the soul goes on into the other world where it abides
until such time as it again becomes incarnate. But such a
view eliminates the personal element in immortality. And
yet that is peculiarly the teaching of Christianity, that the "I"
as an individual shall abide forever, and not merely the impersonal and universal.

---

19. Od. 11:204.
20. Od. 11:488.

Aristotle in this also follows his master. Reason only is immortal and is not individual. The only kind of immortality which Aristotle recognizes is that of the family or race.[21]

A rather strong echo of Plato's teaching is found in certain moderns who ascribe immortality only to those who have lived in accord with the principle of reason within them. The others will perish as do the beasts of the field.

Though the Homeric eschatology was the prevailing belief, among the initiates in the mystery religions there is a hopeful expectation for the future. Aristophanes gives utterance to their expectations in the words, "We alone have the sun and its gladsome light, we who have taken the sacred vow, and have lived a life in the fear of god toward stranger and toward friend."[22] Isocrates says, "Those who share this initiation have sweet hopes for the end of life and for all future time."[23] And Plato says "but he who arrives there after initiation and purification will dwell with the gods."[24] And Cicero writes "In the Mysteries we learn not only to live happily but to die with fairer hope."[25]

On the question of a personal immortality the Mysteries again agreed with Christianity, and because of the similarity on these two points, together with a few others, the two have been declared to be identical. But when inquiry is made as to the means of obtaining or gaining that immortality the two stand far apart. The Mysteries emphasize the sacrament. It is through the rite that the individual is brought into the right relation to God. Every detail of the mystical rite must be carefully observed to reach the desired goal. But Christianity stands at the opposite pole. It is not any rite, but faith which opens the door to the participation in the divine. To be sure, Christianity also had rites and the sacraments.

21. De Anima II, 4, 415a; cf. Nic Ethics 1115a25.
22. Frogs 455-9; cf. Plato's Phaedo 69c.
23. Panegyricus 28.
24. Phaedo 69c; cf. Pindar Frag. 137; Olympian Ode II; Sophocles Frag. 719.
25. De Leg. II. 14.

But in the case of the Mysteries the rite is the efficient thing; in Christianity it is faith, without which the most meticulous observance of the ritual is meaningless.

But there is also a vast difference when the goal or end is considered. In the case of the Mysteries participation in the rite was the means to identification with the divine, or the particular god in whose honor the rite was performed. This was tantamount to a deification of man. Christianity teaches a most intimate union with Christ and God, but never such a union as is equivalent to identification in being. All that Christianity teaches is a spiritual identification so that the whole personality of mind, will, and feelings is one with God and Christ. The Mysteries were much more in accord with Oriental Mysticism, and of a pantheistic character so that the individual is swallowed up again in the all. The Christian view declares that the individual remains and is distinct from the Divine.

In the Christian view of the last things the doctrine of a judgment occupies an important place. The moral outlook in the Old and New Testaments brings it to the fore. But as pronounced as it is in Christian thought so conspicuously absent is it from early Greek thought and life. It came to the fore through Orphic influences. To the average Greek of the classic period it was no more than a poetic fancy. It could hardly be otherwise for the Greek was first of all intellectual and not moral, further he had no real consciousness of sin just because of that, and finally, as has been stated, the soul's existence after death was seriously questioned. One does find a few beautiful and impressive passages in Pindar and Plato.[26]

In the preceding when we were discussing the relation of soul and body, it was said that the Greek attitude toward the body would have a specific effect upon the belief in a resurrec-

---

26. Cf. Gorgias 523ff, Republic 614ff.

tion of the body.[27]   It is evident from the New Testament
that the Greek mind was not sympathetic toward this teaching.[28]   The fact is that for this cardinal doctrine of the New
Testament there is no preparation in Greek religion or philosophy.   Even the Mysteries which proclaimed immortality
had nothing to offer here.   Plato argues seriously for the
immortality of the soul in the Phaedo and Cicero follows him
in the Tusculan Disputations, but the immortality is one of
freedom from the body.   A bodily resurrection was far below
the horizon of any Greek.   The noble Aeschylus has put it
briefly "But when the dust hath drained the blood of man,
when once he has died, there is no return to life."[29]   The word
used is "anastasis" and is more suggestive than "return to
life."

The basis for the contrasting views on this point is found
in the diverging views of the body as was pointed out above.[30]
The Greek sees man as essentially a psychical something.
That constitutes the real man, and that alone is worthy of a
continued existence.   The body is a hindrance to the soul and
therefore perfection can be attained only through a complete
separation from the body.   But the Biblical view is that man
is not merely soul but body also.   The body too constitutes
an essential part of him.   And if that is the case, then the body
too must continue to exist.   There must therefore be a resurrection of the body.   Would it not be a partial redemption
if only the soul were to inherit eternal life?   Paul felt so
keenly that the body is an essential part of man that he would
be "unclothed" without it.[31]   The Greek point of view is
that the highest stage of existence is a state of being rid of
the body.   The Christian view is that man cannot reach the
highest and most complete stage without the body.

27. Cf. p. 136.
28. Cf. Acts 17; I Cor. 15.
29. Eumenides 647-8.
30. Cf. pp. 135-141.
31. II Cor. 5:3.

The Christian teaching on the nature of the resurrection body is a mystery beyond our present knowledge and comprehension. For Paul does not teach the resurrection of the flesh, although many have this conception. Paul's argument does not allow that kind of an interpretation.[32] The body is an organism comparable to a seed. And as the seed dies to produce a different something, so also the body dies, and from it comes a "spiritual body." It has identity with the body but is not flesh. Paul takes a position midway between two extremes. For the Pharisees taught the resurrection of the flesh in immortality. The Greek looked forward only to an immortality of the soul, if he believed in immortality at all. But Paul teaches an immortality in which the body itself shares. And that immortality consists for the body in its becoming spiritual. To be sure no one knows exactly what that is. The picture one can form of it is gained largely through negation. It is not flesh and it does not have the limitations imposed on the flesh by space and time. The resurrected body of Jesus gives the clue. And Paul states emphatically that "flesh and blood shall not inherit the kingdom of heaven."

---

32. I Cor. 15.

CHAPTER XV

Christian and Pagan Ethics

A. *Chief Characteristics*

To MAKE a comparison of the Graeco-Roman world in the field of ethics is very interesting and important. For just here, too, attempts have been made to point out not only similarities but even to argue for the identity of the two. "It has often been asserted that Stoicism was the mediating factor between Christianity and European thought; that the Stoic philosophy was a half-way house to Christianity, and paved the way for the acceptance of Christianity."[1] In the sequel the aim will be to point out that the following statement of Macmurray is much nearer the truth. "Yet the opposite is the truth. Stoicism was the means by which Christianity was corrupted in Europe and side-tracked into dualism."[2] For it is not true that "there was little or no conflict between Christian ethics and those of the Stoics, so that when Christianity found it desirable to state its ethics in systematic form, it proved most convenient for it to adopt that system which had already by experience proved itself best and had commended itself to the good sense of mankind."[3] If the above statement is interpreted strictly as applying to the later history of the church, there is some truth in it. For the fact is that in the early church there was not the full consciousness as to the fundamental disagreement of the two systems. As

---

1. Macmurray, J. — *The Clue to History* p. 138.
2. Ibid. p. 138.
3. Moore, C. H. in Foakes-Jackson ,and Lake — *The Beginnings of Christianity* — vol. I, p. 250.

a consequence there were those who took over the Stoic system almost in its entirety wihtout being aware of the antagonism. But if one takes the statement to apply to the ethical teaching of the New Testament and compares those writings with the expressed views of the Stoics, there will be no agreement. There may at times be a similarity in expression, which on the surface seems to mean the same thing, but upon closer scrutiny and an examination of the whole system turns out to be quite different. So the ideals expressed and the means toward achieving them may appear to be alike, but fundamentally there is disagreement. It has been said that "the Stoic and Pauline ethics agree on the three main points: freedom from the world, conquest of sensuality, and brotherly love."[4] But if it is asked what the content of each of these ideals is, and how they shall be attained the answers are not at all identical. The situation has been summarized in these words: "If Christianity largely absorbed its (Stoicism's) terminology, it invested the terms with an entirely new content, and new values."[5] Or again in these words: "For even where direct contact and resemblance are found to exist, and coincidences of thought and expression are obvious and striking, either the real content of Christianity is not in question, or else the congruous conceptions are in the two cases based upon different principles, and plainly lead to opposite conclusions."[6]

According to some, then, all the really important elements in Christian teaching are found in the ethical writers of pagan antiquity. As an example I would quote: "There was no essential difference between their preaching that men should spend themselves in the service of their fellowmen, and the preaching of Jesus; nor anything new in Jesus' teaching that good should be returned for evil. Even in the field of sexual ethics Paul's austerity was not more than that of his contem-

---

4. Pfleiderer, O. — *Christian Origins*, p. 179.
5. Box, G. H. — Early *Christianity and the Hellenic World* Expositor 1924.
6. Fairweather, W. — *Jesus and the Greeks*, p. 372.

porary saint, Musonius Rufus."[7]   Some of these particulars
will be discussed later.   Suffice it to say at this time that questions as the following must be asked: do the supposed similarities obtain in the field of that which is basic or fundamental
in the Christian view; are the similarities only verbal or is
there agreement in meaning to be attached to the words; are
the means prescribed for attaining the goal, if it is identical,
the same; and finally is the motive the same in both cases.   It
is the purpose here to point out the marked difference between
the two in the fundamental concepts and attitudes, and also in
the specific virtues.   And it will be seen that the contrast reveals itself not only in what was held up positively as the
ideal, but also and especially in some fundamental omissions
on the part of Greek thought.   The ethics of Plato, Aristotle,
and the Stoics did have a profound influence on the early
Church, but their ethics is not that of Jesus, Paul, and John.

Before entering upon a more detailed investigation of
specific elements a few introductory remarks must be made.
First of all a word about the history of Greek ethics.   Some
writers, as Thomas H. Green, have written as though the
highest level of ethical thought was reached in Aristotle, and
that the ethics of today is practically that of Aristotle with
the qualification that it has been widened and expanded.   But
it must not be forgotten that great advances were made after
Aristotle, especially by the Stoics.   Various writers have indicated this advance.   Thus More has written: "If there is
originality in this branch of the Stoic ethics it is in the change
from the Aristotelian method of defining virtue by some rule
of measure in the activities themselves to this consideration
of right conduct as determined by man's relations with other
men.   Here, as in other respects, Stoicism holds a curious
halfway position between paganism and Christanity."[8]   And
Spence goes a step further, "There was emphatically something in their teaching loftier, purer, more real than had ever

---

7. Dorsey, G. A. — *Man's Own Show*, p. 534.
8. More, P. E. — *Hellenistic Philosophies*, p.119.

appeared before in the teaching of any pagan philosophic schools."[9] Lightfoot gives the Stoics great credit for their emphasis on conscience, and writes "the most important of moral terms, the crowning triumph of ethical nomenclature, suneidesis, the internal, absolute, supreme judge of individual action, if not struck in the mint of the Stoics, at all events became current coin through their influence."[10] In comparison with them Aristotle stands far below. It is just because of these advances in Stoicism that men are tempted to see practical identity between it and Christianity.

Further it is noteworthy that morality occupies such a supremely important place in the teaching of the New Testament. Here, of course, we see the genuine Hebrew spirit manifesting itself as over against the Greek. For if one were to single out one of the greatest weaknesses of pagan antiquity it would be exactly in the field of morals, both as to the place it occupied and the specific virtues or lack of virtues. For throughout antiquity there is no real, vital bond between religion and morality. Just where Christianity is strong, the pagan world was weak. Because God according to the Hebrew-Christian tradition is an ethical being, and the highest ideal of perfection, it was imperative that those who sought and professed fellowship with Him strive after the same things. But beginning with Homer, Greek religion did not inculcate the highest of morals. The Homeric pantheon can not be described as living on high moral ground. The gods are supermen, with more power and wisdom, but hardly with more noble ethical ideals and practices. Olympus had human life lifted to the top of a mountain, but retaining its essential weaknesses of deceit, falsehood, quarreling, immorality. And this Homeric mythology continued to be the dominant influence in Greek and Roman life. The Mysteries lifted to somewhat higher ground. But even there

9. Spence, D. M. — *Early Christianity and Paganism,* p. 172.
10. Lightfoot, J. B. — *St. Paul and Seneca,* p. 287 in "Dissertations on the Apostolic Age."

one does not find the absolutely close relation of religion and morality. For there is no essential connection between the rite performed and the moral life. And reversely we find philosophers teaching morality, but not religion. The two simply were not bound together inseparably, and in such a relation that true religion alone becomes the foundation of true morals.

The same phenomenon continues through the Hellenistic age. Religion had no power to make men moral, nor had it any high ethical ideals. And it was exactly at this point that ancient paganism saw the sharpest of contrasts between itself and Christianity. For Jesus, following the teaching of the Old Testament, laid down the precept, "Be ye holy as your father in heaven is holy." That necessarily affected the whole moral outlook. Therein is given an absolute standard and criterion. Faith without works is declared to be dead. Fellowship with Jesus and the Divine can only be genuine when it expresses itself in high moral ideals and life. Accordingly Christianity even declares itself to be a way of life.[11] And Paul most emphatically insists on a life of purity and holiness.

Although lacking a true basis for morals because it had no truly high and worthy religion, the Hellenistic Age is characterized by an emphasis on conduct. In this respect both the dominant philosophies of Zeno and Epicureus are at one. To be sure the means to be employed are radically different, as will be pointed out later. But what among other things characterized this age was an interest in and application to the questions of conduct. It seems that the mind was weary of idle speculations about the invisible and the impractical. Hence a turning to the immediate questions of how men ought to live. In that sense philosophy has now become a way of life. The philosophies are akin to the Socratic which brought its speculations down from the heavens to earth. That ac-

---

11. Acts 2:28; 9:2; 19:9; 24:22.

counts for the fact that the followers of Plato were by no means the most numerous and influential in the Hellenistic Age. Theorizing about the world of ideas had not brought happiness and prosperity. Therefore men turned to that which lay nearer at hand and seemed to offer a quicker and more sound solution. The chief interest lay in the field of ethics. But though weariness and futility have contributed something to this it is not the full explanation. In a preceding chapter (Chapter IV) it was pointed out that Zeno and the original Stoic movement was of a Semitic character, which concerned itself essentially with the problems of deeds, actions, and morals generally. The Semitic mind put such problems first and did not concern itself essentially with the problems of ultimate reality. That is quite evident from the Stoic philosophy in which small consideration is given to such questions as the ultimate nature of the universe. Indeed, their theory of elemental fire formed a background to other theories, but it remained only a background. But this Stoic philosophy becomes practical especially because it has passed over to Roman soil. The Romans were neither gifted for abstract speculation nor were they interested. Essentially they were men of deeds, very practical in their attitudes and interests. They took over the ethical speculations of the Greeks and then concerned themselves especially with the application of these theories.

In the process they naturally absorbed many of the distinctive elements of Greek thought. First of all these is the intellectualism of the Greeks. It can readily be seen that if the essential nature of man was as the Greek viewed him, he was bound to have an intellectualistic attitude toward morals and life. And that is exactly what we find from Socrates down through the generations. It passed on into Rome, was largely submerged for a time in the Christian civilization of the Middle Ages, but reasserted itself with the Revival of Learning, and since then has dominated the life of the Western world. Because the point is extremely important, striking at the very foundation of our attitudes toward life, an effort must be put forth to make the position clear.

Every one knows that Socrates affirmed that the "Unexamined life is not worth living for man." That meant a careful and ceaseless examination of all his beliefs and practices. Nothing should be accepted or done because of tradition or habit, but all must be grounded on solid arguments of reason. Now it is true that with all his intellectualism Socrates had something of the mystic in him. How else explain his absolute obedience to the daimonion which spoke at times without any apparent rational explanation? Or again how explain his enraptured hours of contemplation when he was lost to the external world round about him?

But the fact is that especially his intellectual views were understood and accepted. Down through the generations men declared like Socrates that Knowledge is Virtue. Its corollary, already for Socrates, was that no man does evil voluntarily. If his conduct is evil it must be that he does not know what he is doing. Increased and improved knowledge will overcome his present wickedness.

Plato and later philosophers continued in the same general direction, and declared the same fundamental truths in different words. It has been pointed out above that the real part of man is his intelligence, his mind. Throughout the writings of Plato we find that repeated emphasis. This intellectualism of the Greeks manifests itself even in the tragedies in what strikes us as almost a bit humorous. One character greets another on the stage as "Dear Head."   And in a passage in Plato we read, "I love you from the bottom of my mind."[12] One reads such statements and is inclined to pass them by without thought, because in the tragedies they are merely the introduction to a further remark. But when one reflects, he asks how is it that the Greek should so address

---

12. Gorg. 510c.

another? Is there not a real reason for it? And is not that reason at variance with the Christian position? Do we not greet in an altogether different way? It is not "dear head" but "dear heart." In those expressions the whole difference of fundamental outlook is expressed.

The Greek was intellectualistic. The head was the real man. This is so much the case in Plato that according to him the head alone is immortal. But all the chief philosophies of antiquity took the same position. In Stoicism especially does this intellectualism assert itself strongly. Seneca writes, "What then is peculiar to man? Reason. When this is right and has reached perfection, man's felicity is complete."[13] Specifically He says, "Reason, however, is nothing else than a portion of the divine spirit in a human body."[14] This glorification and deification of the intellect explains the emphases of pagan morals. And that too accounts for the omission of the specific Christian virtues. Read Plato, Aristotle, Marcus Aurelius, Epictetus, Seneca, Cicero, and one finds, not withstanding noble and true sentiments, that the basis is different, and that the virtues extolled are not the same, or are not extolled for the same reason.

If it be true that the intellect occupies such a prominent place, then there are specific consequences for the scale of virtues, as well as for the whole life of man. Aristotle regards all moral virtues as only a kind of porch and access to the contemplative life, in which man truly reaches his goal, as does God. Only then when the intellect has reached its peak, can man be said to be truly happy. Man must therefore take reason as his guide and regulate his life according to it. Thus did all the philosophers, Socrates, Plato, Aristotle, the Stoics teach.

Because the point is so extremely important it is well to indicate a few of the consequences of this over-emphasis of

---

13. Ep. Mor. LXXVI, 10.
14. Ep. Mor. LXVI, 12.

the intellect. This will serve to bring out in sharp relief the Christian view. The outstanding consequence is that the chief of the virtues is an intellectual one. Because man is essentially mind, and through the proper functioning of the mind man attains his goal of happiness, therefore the highest virtue must be something which is the result of the active mind. Among the four cardinal virtues of antiquity wisdom occupies the highest place. It could not be otherwise. Already in the early poets there were suggestions of these cardinal virtues of wisdom, temperance, courage, and justice. Plato merely brings them out in bold relief in his dialogues.[15] Aristotle follows in his steps, and in the Stoics we find the same thing. "And then," says Cicero, "the foremost of all virtues is wisdom — what the Greeks call sophia."[16] Paul recognized this as distinguishing the Greeks for they seek wisdom.[17] But the New Testament clearly teaches that the foremost virtue is "love." The fulfilling of the law consists in "love." "Thou shalt love the Lord the God with all thy heart, and with all thy soul, and with all thy mind. This is the first and great commandment. And a second like unto it is this, Thou shalt love thy neighbor as thyself."[18] Nevertheless the cardinal virtues of antiquity passed over into the Church and greatly influenced some of its teachers. They formed a central point in the teaching of Origen, and Ambrose devotes considerable space to them.[19] Ambrose, in turn, greatly influenced St. Augustine and he again influenced Acquinas. Ambrose' work on the Duties of the Clergy follows Cicero very closely, so that he discusses at length the cardinal virtues, but gives no separate treatment to the Christian triad of faith, hope, and love. In outlining these duties he says, "First thou shalt see the deep things of God, which needs wisdom. Next thou

15. Prot. 329c; Meno 78d; Gorg. 507b; Rep. 427e.
16 De Officiis I, XLIII, 153.
17. I Cor. 1:22.
18. Matt. 22:37-38.
19. Duties of Clergy I-II.

must keep watch for the people; this requires justice. Thou must defend the camp, and guard the tabernacle, which needs fortitude. Thou must show thyself continent and sober, and this needs temperance."[20]

The inevitable consequences of such over-emphasis on the intellect is that virtue in the real and highest sense will be found in only a few. For if complete insight and understanding determine the ethical value of a deed, then only rare souls will attain the heights. For comparatively few have the ability to rise to such clear insight. The system of morals then is not something for the masses since they are not able to reach the goal of intellectual comprehension. Therein lies the weakness of the systems of ethics of ancient paganism. They were if good, only for a few. The "wise man" was something far away and above the reach of the common man. In this intellectualism therefore lay the sterility of the ancient ethics.

If the ideal of virtuous action is to be found in clear understanding, then all acts in which such understanding is not present, fall short of the truly virtuous. Socrates had taught very clearly that knowledge is virtue, that an unexamined life is not worthy of man. All else, however good, is not really virtuous. The consequence is one that forms the sharpest contrast with the Christian view. In it the unconscious instinct to do good receives its proper reward, and is regarded as virtuous. "But when the Son of man shall come in his glory, and all the angels with him, then shall he sit on the throne of his glory; and before him shall be gathered all the nations: and he shall separate them one from another, as the shepherd separateth the sheep from the goats; and he shall set the sheep on his right hand, but the goats on the left. Then shall the king say unto them on his right hand, Come, ye blessed of my Father, inherit the kingdom prepared for you from the foundation of the world: for I was hungry and ye gave me to eat; I was thirsty, and ye gave me drink; I was

20. Duties of Clergy I, L, 260.

a stranger and ye took me in; naked, and ye clothed me; I
was sick, and ye visited me; I was in prison, and ye came unto
me.   Then shall the righteous answer him, saying, Lord,
when saw we thee hungry, and fed thee: or athirst, and gave
thee drink?   And when saw we thee a stranger, and took thee
in? or naked, and clothed thee?   And when saw we thee
sick, or in prison, and came unto thee?   And the King shall
answer and say unto them, Verily I say unto you, Inasmuch
as ye did it unto one of these my brethren, even these least, .
ye did it unto me."[21]

These acts of kindness and mercy had been performed in-
stinctively and had therefore been forgotten by the doers.   But
according to the teaching of Jesus the very fact that the deeds
had been done by instinct makes them worthy of eternal reward.   The difference between the view of Jesus and that of
pagan antiquity is very great.   But the same view has come
down into modern times.   The Earl of Shaftesbury argued
that virtue, as distinguished from mere goodness, is impossible without reflection.[22]   Kant agrees with this intellectualism of antiquity.[23]   For he took the position, contrary to the
teaching of Jesus, that actions which are prompted only by
a good-natured temperament have no moral value.   And he
came dangerously close to the Socratic dictum that Knowledge is Virtue when he ascribed the evil that men do to their
irrational character rather than to their ungodly nature.   Therefore, if men are made more rational, they will also become
more virtuous.

A peculiar application of this intellectualism is seen in the
case of Plato when he discusses the nature of the lie.[24]   To all
who have a Christian outlook the lie consists in the uttered
word contrary to the representation of the truth within.   But
not so Plato. The great, the real lie is not that which is uttered

21. Matt. 25:31-40.
22. Shaftebury, Earl of: Inquiry Concerning Virtur I, Pt. II, Sec. III.
23. Cf. Stewart, J. A.: Notes on Nic. Ethics Vol. I, p. 201.
24. Rep 382a-c.

in words, but is to be found within in the state of ignorance.
The veritable "lie" in the case of Plato is found in a lack of
true thinking. The "lie" is in the soul and not in the words.
The other is not a real "lie" because it is only an utterance of
the lips. This sets the Christian view topsy-turvy, and leads
to a strange view of the nature of evil. Because the essence
of virture lies in the intellect, in other words in a state of
knowing, it is declared to be better, or more virtuous to do
evil knowingly, than to be virtuous without knowledge.

This all leads to a further consequence. Virtue is, as has
been said, a matter of knowledge. But just because of this
over-emphasis of the intellect there always was great possibility of misuse of the mind. Life became a contest of wits,
and cleverness became the guage instead of goodness. Since
mind was the highest in man, and its functioning the gauge
of approach to the ideal, any activity of the intellect, as long
as it revealed brilliance and alertness, was regarded as reaching
toward the goal. Hence we find that mere cleverness was
the criterion of actions, and not goodness.

Further, the real explanation of the "mean" in Greek ethics
is to be found in this intellectualism. For virtue consists in
a very careful calculation, which is a functioning of the intellect. Though this doctrine of the "mean" found classic presentation in Aristotle it by no means is his discovery. Rather
was it a natural outgrowth of the general characteristic of
moderation in the Greeks. And in various passages Plato
has anticipated all that is of real value in Aristotle's doctrine.[25] The doctrine of the "mean" characterizes itself as
opposed to all excess, and the determining thing is the intellect which carefully weighs the conditions, and consequences.
It therefore becomes something of a prudential ethics. And
whatever the good may be in such a conception of virtue,
there is an inevitable weakness. Genuine enthusiasm, a com-

---

25. Pol. 283e-284a, 284d, 306aff, 310. Cf. Theactetus 144a; Rep. 375c,
410d, 503c; Laws 731b, 773b: Cf. Stewart, J. A.: Notes on Nic. Ethics vol.
I, p. 196.

pelling and controlling passion in life is necessarily eliminated. The virtuous life becomes cool, calculating, and misses the height of zeal and warmth.

A further manifestation of this intellectualism lies in the position occupied by the will and the emotions. It is interesting to note that Christianity transfers the emphasis from the intellect to the will, or rather to the heart. The Greek systems and the Stoic were lofty in conception, but lacked the dynamic necessary for the truly ethical life. These systems were aflicted with sterility, just because of their intellectualism. But Christian teaching succeeds where these philosophic systems had failed, because the emphasis was no longer put on the mind.[26]

The Greek taught that ignorance is the sole cause of the lack of virtue. Man therefore, must be enlightened. Knowledge, said Socrates, is virtue. They never questioned the ability and strength of the will to do good. The terrific struggle which Paul describes as being waged within himself the Greek did not know, "For that which I do, I know not; for not what I would, that do I practice; but what I hate, that I do. But if what I would not, that I do, I consent unto the law, that it is good. So now it is no more I that do it, but sin which dwelleth in me. For I know that in me, that is, in my flesh, dwelleth no good thing: for to will is present with me, but to do that which is good is not. For the good which I would I do not; but the evil which I would not, that I do. But if what I would not that I do it is no more I that do it, but sin which dwelleth in me. I find then the law, that, to me who would do good, evil is present. For I delight in the law of God after the inward man: but I see a different law in my members, warring aginst the law of my mind, and bringing me into captivity under the law of sin which is in my members. Wretched man that I am! Who shall deliver me out of the body

---

26. More, P. E.: Hellenistic Philosophies p. 299. Cf. Niebuhr, R.: An Interpretation of Christian Ethics, p. 206.

of this death."[27] Here then the contrast is complete. According to Paul there is something in himself more powerful than that which he knows. His wretched state is not due to lack of knowledge, but lack of will. The Greek had taught that the whole weakness of man lay in his not knowing, and that if only he know, his will was strong enough and would follow the direction laid out by the mind. But Paul teaches that though there is right knowledge, yet his will is utterly unable to attain.[28]

The point is extremely important, for on it will depend whether one follows out in his ethics the Christian position or will fall back on the pagan. St. Augustine followed more in the line of Paul and made man essentially "will,"[29] and thereby took position against the view of antiquity. But modern idealism again elevated the intellect of man and made him essentially a "thinker" and thereby has again fallen back on the position of the pagans.[30] Among the ancients Aristotle displays something of insight into the importance of will by his emphasis on discipline and habit, but it by no means occupies the important position it does in Christian teaching.

The direct consequence is that one of the characteristic elements of Christianity, namely regeneration, is missing from Graeco-Roman thought. "Ye must be born again," resounds through the pages of the New Testament. As it was confounding to Nicodemus, so it is beyond the grasp of the Greek. There are to be sure, indications that something quite radical must happen to man. But that radical transformation takes place in the mind of man because that is the chief element in him. In the so-called allegory of the cave Plato has an important passage in which he speaks of this regeneration. "Whereas, I said, our argument shows that the power is al-

---

27. Rom. 7:15-24.
28. Cf. Bultmann, R.: Der Stil der Paul. Predigt und die kynisch-stoische Diatribe. p. 85.
29. City of God XIV, 6.
30. Means, S.: Faith p. 334.

ready in the soul; and that as the eye cannot turn from darkness to light without the whole body, so too, when the eye of the soul is turned around, the whole soul must be turned from the world of generation into that of being, and become able to endure the sight of being, and of the brightest and best of being — that is to say, of the good.

Very true.

And this is conversion; and the art will be how to accomplish this as easily and completely as possible; not implanting eyes, for they exist already, but giving them a right direction, which they have not.

"Yes," he said, "that may be assumed."

And hence, while the other qualities seem to be akin to the body, being infused by habit and exercise and not originally innate, the virtue of wisdom is part of divine essence, and has a power whch is everlasting, and by this conversion is rendered useful and profitable, and is also capable of becoming hurtful and useless."[31]

Now this passage brings out the typically Greek view in two respects. First the conversion is above all intellectual. Man must be turned to comprehend the Good with his mind.[32] But enough has been said on that point. The second thing of importance is that this conversion is purely human. There is no super-natural element in it. Because the soul is divine there is no need of the super-natural entering into it. But the distinctive thing about Christian teaching is exactly that it does not ascribe to the natural spirit of man the ability to arrive at the vision of the truth by its own efforts. Hence, the conversion is an entering into man of the supernatural world through Christ, and that consists in much more than intellectual enlightenment. The constant teaching of Plato, Aristotle, the Stoics is that the remedy for moral disease is education. But Christianity declares that there is need of a conversion of

31. Rep. 518-19.
32. Hutton, M.: The Greek Point of View, p. 26.

one's whole being, and that this is brought about only by a power higher and greater than man.

This discussion of the intellectualism of the ancients has been rather extended because of its great importance. For had the ancient system died at the birth of Christianity, or certainly at the end of the third century after Christ there would be little need of long discussion. But the fact is that this view has maintained through the centuries. It has been pointed out how completely St. Ambrose accepted the ancient system. And at the beginning of modern thought one finds a complete resurgence of it. Modern philosophy begins with Descartes who had utter trust in reason. And the "Age of Enlightenment," also called the "Age of Reason" is a perfect parallel to the life of the Stoics. For both had boundless confidence in the power of the mind. Mercier has stated it clearly: "It is but the culmination of the neo-stoical movement which begins with the Renaissance and tends to imbue man again with the ancient Stoics' proud confidence of being able to achieve virtue through knowledge."[33]

A second important trait is the emphasis on the individual. Now it may seem strange that this is pointed out as a contrast with the Christian view. For surely Christian ethics stands out exactly on this point of the worth of the individual. The difference in point of view is not, however, as to the ultimate worth but the attitude which the individual takes toward himself and others, and as a result the completely different teaching on how the individual is best to realize himself. More will be said about this later when discussing the virtue of humility, and again when the attitude toward one's fellow man is taken up. It will suffice here to indicate in the man the difference in point of view.

Pagan ethics can be described as self-centered. The virtues are treated as states of the virtuous man. And ancient ethics has a strong tendency to regard man as in a vacuum.

33. Mercier, L.: Challenge of Humanism, p. 28.

His virtues are those qualities which he possesses and practises as though there were no other individuals. At best his virtue extended only to the bounds of his fellow citizens, and even among them the weak were ignored. The whole scheme of things is radically different from the Christian which emphasizes love, and the neighbor. Especially Epicureanism and Stoicism took extreme positions. The ideal was to be attained by withdrawal from all contacts with one's fellowmen. It consisted in a proud self-sufficiency. Man must live within himself, for he is entirely sufficient unto himself. "The self-centered, almost haughty aristocratic righteousness of the good man, the just citizen, the noble patriot, the loving friend, and true seeker after truth in Plato's dialogues seems cold and beautiful as a Grecian marble, compared to the loving gentleness of the Christian ideal."[34] In the case of pagan ethics the ideal is detachment, separation from all the world outside, a living in and by oneself alone because he is sufficient unto all things, while the Christian ideal is incorporation because love is the controlling force. The Christian loses himself in the service of others, gives himself completely. Everything in the pagan conception centers about the "self." Therefore in Greek thought there is no virtue of "duty" nor is there even a word for it. The ideal is the "good," but even that is something self-regarding.[35] One's obligations toward his fellow-man were restricted to his fellow citizens, and then only so far as these were laid down in the law. There was no "special claim on the part of the weak, the oppressed, the sick, the suffering, the poor. The duties of Philanthropy, of Almsgiving, of Mercy are simply non-existent in the elaborate enumeration of virtues and duties given us by Aristotle. Neither Mercy, nor any equivalent of it appears in Aristotle's very detailed list of virtues; the nearest he gets to it is in Equity which is only a higher form of justice."[36] In short the Chris-

34. Hall: T. C.: History of Christian Ethics, p. 84.
35. Hutton, M.: Greek Point of View, p. 59.
36. Rashdall, H.: Conscience and Christ, p. 82 ff.

tian view is that man shall save his life by losing it, by merging himself in the life of others, by surrender of the self to the whole. In the case of Stoicism we are here confronted with a strange paradox. For on the one hand it insisted on brotherhood and social service, but on the other hand advocated an isolation for the wise man which nullified its teaching of relationship with one's fellowman.[37]

A further trait of pagan ethics was its humanism. At this point we again find the Christian view which is based on the Old Testament at variance with the pagan. For all the Orientals, Israel included, had a different conception of the origin of law from that which was held by the Greeks. In the East law is a divine revelation, and hence comes from a source that is more than human. There is in it, therefore, the element of unalterableness. The rule for behavior becomes absolute. But in Greece the laws are made by men, and are regarded as human. On the surface the consequence of this would be that these laws might therefore be set aside or transgressed easily by the individual. Such a view was taken by the Sophists and later by the Cynics. The former loved to speak of the contrast and contradiction between law and nature. Law signified to them largely mere convention and custom. And these were at variance with nature. But the great stream of Greek thought did not flow in that channel. To their minds law was something sacred and binding, not because of its super-human origin, but because it was the voice of the people, and that voice spoke loudly because it was greater than that of any individual. Plato said that the laws are not as "tyrants and masters who command and threaten and after writing their decrees on walls go their way."[38] but they reason with men and seek to win their consent.

This conception of law and its nature rests upon the Greek view of man as fundamentally a rational being. When the

---

37. Inge, W. R.: Outspoken Essays Vol. II, p. 47.
38. Laws 859a.

people in conclave express themselves and express these utterances in laws, they are therefore the expression of man's rational character. Consequently no one individual may lightly set himself against or transgress the laws. These laws are the expression of the collective reason of the people. It is therefore utter folly for an individual to stand over against that with his own particular reason. For reason must ultimately be one, and it expresses itself through the group. It is sheer absurdity to think that each man has a private reason, belonging to himself alone and contrary to the corporate reason of the people.[39] The Greek, therefore, had great respect and reverence for law because it was the voice of the people. And that law was regarded as almost divine, because man's reason is divine. Nevertheless this is pure humanism because man only is its author and source. Over against such teaching stands that of the Old Testament which declares that the law is the utterance of God himself. There is in the law, therefore, something essentially superhuman and genuinely divine. That conception of law has passed over into the New Testament. This law of God himself must be carried out in all of one's behaviour. It becomes the norm and criterion of virtue. According to it man must conduct his life.

Not so the Greek. His guide becomes "Nature." But what is "Nature?" The term requires careful definition. For at times it refers to the nature of the individual man as the standard. This leads back to Protagoras who declared that man is the measure of all things. And though he may have meant it in a collective sense there can be no doubt that many in Greece took it in an entirely individualistic one. In such a case the individual man is called upon to use and to follow the intelligence which he has as the final standard. This view is a natural logical consequence when one admits that the mind of man is something divine.

---

39. Earp. F. R.: The Way of the Greeks. p. 138.

But a broader conception of "nature" is that which includes the universe. In the world there resides reason or logos, and man shares in it. Because of it man has great respect for the laws laid down by his fellowmen, as was indicated above. The guidance for man's life is therefore to be found in this reason resident in himself and the universe generally. "Follow nature" was the slogan of Greeks and Stoics, for in nature herself there is something divine. The two elements of "nature" though seemingly at variance, agree in that both view nature whether in man or the universe as divine. In fact man is but a part of the great universe itself.

A few quotations from Stoic writers will serve to make the point clear. Cicero has great confidence in nature and writes, "If we follow nature as our guide, we shall never go astray, but we shall be pursuing that which is in its nature clear-sighted and penetrating (Wisdom) that which is adapted to promote and strengthen society (Justice) and that which is strong and courageous (Fortitude)."[40] And again, "When the Stoics speak of the supreme good as 'living conformably to nature' they mean, as I take it, something like this: that we are always to be in accord with virtue, and from all other things that may be in harmony with nature to choose only such as are not incompatible with nature."[41] Seneca says, "For we must use nature as our guide; she it is that reason heeds, it is of her that it takes counsel."[42]

It is characteristic of Christian teaching that the standard of conduct is to be found in something above nature. For the Christian view is that "nature" neither as applied to man nor as applied to the universe can serve as the standard. Man's nature is corrupt and sinful. And the universe groans under the consequences of sin.[43] It is an easy optimism which regards "nature" so highly that it can become the guide for life.

---

40. De Officiis Bk. I, Chap. XXVIII, 100.
41. De Officiis III, III 13; cf. III, VIII, 35.
42. De Beata Vita VIII, 1; cf. III, 3 and De Providentia IV, 15.
43. Rom. 8:22 cf. Gardner, P.: Religious Experience of St. Paul p. 142.

Although nature does teach certain things as power, wisdom, she falls short in making known exactly the virtues taught by Christianity, about which we shall speak in the next chapter. Therefore the Christian turns to God for his standard. "To Hebrew and Christian ethics God is the measure."[44] Pagan antiquity was satisfied with humanistic standards, with the experience and history of man, but Christian thought rises to the height of God himself. The Christian is called to be holy as his Father in heaven is holy. The standard for achieving that holiness is found in the Law and the Gospel which are God-given. There is therefore in Christian ethic a totally different emphasis. Man must conduct himself not according to the light within himself, nor according to the light he can discern in the universe round about him, but according to the Light which comes from above man and nature, from the God of Light himself. His life becomes therefore, not mere development of what is within nor mere adjustment to what is about him, but a transformation of all relationships according to the pattern laid down in the Word, and lived by Christ Jesus. Above, in the chapters on God, and Man, it was pointed out that God is Spirit (pneuma) and that man reborn is a spiritual being. The aim of life is therefore to become filled with that Spirit, who is God himself, and to become like Christ. It need hardly be pointed out that the ideal of antiquity (conformity to nature) remains at best an abstraction, while in Christian teaching the goal is a person, both Christ and God.[45]

Paul took cognizance of this Stoic view when he speaks of the heathen that "they do by nature the things of the law,"[46] and again when he refers to "things which are not fitting,"[47] to indicate that man is without excuse. It is remarkable how closely Ambrose followed the pagan view. He wrote, "At the same time let us note that it is seemly to live in accordance

44. Du Bose: The Gospel in the Gospels, p. 104.
45. Ottley, R. L.: Christian Ideas and Ideals, p. 43.
46. Rom. 2:14.
47. Rom. 1:28.

with nature and to pass our time in accordance with it, and that whatever is contrary to nature is shameful."[48]   Again he says, "For if a virtuous life is in accordance with nature — for God made all things very good — then shameful living must be opposed to it."[49]   In more recent times Dr. Samuel Johnson said, "The way to be happy is to live according to nature, in obedience to that universal and unalterable law with which every heart is originally impressed, which is not written on it by precept, but engraven by destiny, not instilled by education, but infused at our nativity.   He that lives according to nature will suffer nothing from delusions of hope or importunities of desire; he will receive and reject with equability of temper, and act or suffer as the reason of things shall alternately prescribe.   To live according to nature is to act always with regard to the fitness arising from the relations of causes and effects; to concur with the great and unchangeable scheme of universal felicity; to cooperate with the general disposition and tendency of the present system of things."[50] In that quotation there is nothing but ancient Stoicism, and many moderns have advanced not a whit over the ancients.

------

48. Duties of the Clergy, I, XLVI; cf. I, 115, 116.
49. Idem. III, IV.
50. Quoted by Fairweather, W.: Jesus and the Greeks, p. 381.

CHAPTER XVI

Christian and Pagan Ethics

B. *The Virtues*

I N T H E last chapter the fundamental differences between Christian and pagan ethics were considered. We now turn to a consideration of the virtues in order to observe more particularly the manifestation of those fundamental points of view. For a detailed investigation only will bring out the points of similarity and disagreement.

In the preceding pages it has already been mentioned that the ideal of antiquity consisted of the four virtues of wisdom, courage, temperance and justice. The Christian triad of virtues is faith, hope, and love. Are these three to be regarded as supplanting the four? Or are they merely to be added to the virtues of the ancients? Do the fundamental Christian virtues express the same ideas as the ancient quatrad though it be in other terms? Or is there a different conception of life, its meaning and its obligations?

There is no doubt that much new territory has been taken in by the Christian conception. Some time ago it was stated "To the four moral virtues which comprehended the whole moral world to the heathen eye, and which have for their sphere of action the relations of men with each other — there have been added the three virtues of faith, hope, and charity, the object of which is God. That was a revolution of the whole man."[1]

A little reflection on these two groups of four and three virtues brings to the foreground certain differences. The car-

---

1. Allies, T. W. — *Formation of Christendom* Vol. I, p. 202.

dinal virtues of the ancients are at times described as being more masculine and virile than the Christian. Nietzsche in his violent antipathy to Christianity sensed this keenly. As a result he regarded Christian ethics those of the weaklings and downtrodden. They arose from the fact that Israel was a subject people, cringing before the power of Rome, and therefore taught humility, meekness, and patience as befitting a conquered people. It is interesting to note that in various so-called Christian lands there is today a rebirth of this same attitude. An extreme nationalism emphasizes today those qualities in men which are not distinctly Christian. The situation becomes even more serious when science comes to the aid of these fundamentally barbaric and unchristian views. For psychoanalysis emphasizes that "the virtues of meekness, humility, long-suffering, gentleness compassion, and so forth, are to be replaced by the more positive sentiments of self-assertion, confidence, boldness, courage. If we would be mentally healthy, we are advised to be forceful."[2]

There is a measure of truth in the characterization given above, for the ancient are essentially the masculine virtues, as they were manifested in and for the state. The virtues are the result of the peculiar position of men and women in ancient civilization, and can therefore at the same time be viewed as an index of and a reflection on that civilization. In it man occupied the center of the stage and woman was pushed into the background. The virtuous life therefore was described in terms of what was befitting the ideal man in such a society. But the Christian virtues describe what is befitting for all, male and female, bond and free. The Christian point of view is therefore more inclusive because its virtues hold for all, but also because they rise above the merely human level and link up with God. Faith, hope, and love span time and reach eternity and the infinite. The ancient virtues rest on the fundamental assumption that man is essentially intel-

---

2. Barbour, C. E. — *Sin and the New Psychology,* p. 193.

ligence. The virtues are therefore manifestations of a reasonable attitude. The Christian virtues rest on man's nature as "spiritual" and therefore take that character. It has been strongly stated "that the pagan virtues are the reasonable, and that the Christian virtues are in essence as unreasonable as they can be."[3] Because of its intellectualism and its self-centeredness Greek ethics could not but be a system which emphasized that all must accord with reason, and, that reason rests in the individual.

But the charge that the Christian virtues are those of weaklings over against the strong, and therefore are essentially weak is open to many attacks. For although the Christian system does not exalt "courage" as one of its cardinal virtues, that does not mean that the Christian lacks courage. The term among the ancients had various meanings ranging from the manifestation of instinctive impulses in the direction of destroying by force an opposing force to the highest form of contending for the good in the ideal life. Usually it applied to the devotion of the soldier in defense of his fellow-citizens and the state. In the Christian ethics the follower of Christ is called upon to resist evil and the world in the face of opposition, criticism, and ridicule. In the face of that to continue steadfast in the faith requires courage. And surely in the early history of the church the Christian was called upon to display real courage in behalf of his belief. The fact of the matter is that the term among the Greeks was too narrowly limited to the task of a soldier fighting for his state, and therefore could not be retained in the Christian vocabulary with the same emphasis and frequency. The virtue of courage is replaced by that of patience which bears with fortitude the shocks and changes of life because of implicit faith in the providence of God.[4] That type of courage is not weaker than that manifested temporarily on the battle-

---

3. Chesterton, G. K. — "Paganism and Mr. Lowes Dickinson" in *The Greek Genius and its Influence*, p. 271.
4. Ottley, R. L.: Christian Ideas and Ideals, pp. 185-187.

field. The Christian system in this respect far outshines its
contemporaries, Epicureanism and Stoicism, which both manifested a lack of true courage for the battle of life by their
insistence on withdrawal into the self, away from and above
the turmoil of life.

A second characteristic is the emphasis put upon the inner
attitude in the Christian system. The contrast is well put in
these words, "he (Aristotle) is wholly incapable of conceiv-
ing that a man may be liberal who has little or nothing to
give. The saying of the widow's mite is quite beyond his ken."[5]
In the mind of Aristotle true virtue must express itself in
the act as well as well as the intention, and great stress is put
upon the act itself.   In the Christian view the inner attitude
is all important.   "The great characteristic of Christian morality is 'inwardness.' "[6]

When the apostle declares that the greatest of the Christian
triad is love the emphasis is shifted from the realm of the
intellect to include that of feeling and will. As over against
the narrow intellectualism of the Greeks the apostle places
the whole man. For certainly no one could think that Paul
is anti-intellectual. His letters clearly demonstrate the contrary for there is emphasis on the need of instruction in and
of understanding the faith.   But his entire outlook is not
limited to the mind, but centers in the heart, or if you will,
the emotions and will of man. That too becomes the seat
of the virtuous life. Man is not primarily intelligence, but
is spirit (pneuma), and his essential activity is therefore one
of the spirit. There had been faint suggestions that the will
was supremely important but these were not followed up and
thought through. Aristotle, by his emphasis on discipline
and habit had hold of the matter in essence, but apparently
did not follow it out. But Christianity definitely transferred

---

5. Rashdall, H. — *Conscience and Christ,* p. 102.
6. Ottley, R. L. — Christian Ideas and Ideals, p. 118.

the source of good and evil to the heart, and made strong appeal to the emotions.[7]

Before leaving this point it may be well to indicate by a few snatches from history the influence of this intellectualism of the Greek attitude. Because it was so universal one could hardly expect that the early Church would be free from it. It is interesting to note how Athenagoras has completely imbibed its spirit for he maintains that the understanding is the means of knowing God. He says, "But to us, who distinguish God from matter, and teach that matter is one thing and God another, and that they are separated by a wide interval (for that the Deity is uncreated and eternal, to be beheld by the understanding and reason alone, while matter is created and perishable) is it not absurd to apply the name of atheism?"[8] St. Ambrose can hardly escape the criticism of placing the intellect first, for it functions in all the virtues. "What duty connected with the chief virtues was wanting in these men (Jacob, Joseph, Job, David). In the first place they showed prudence, which is exercised in the search of truth, and which imparts a desire for full knowledge; next justice, which assigns each man his own, does not claim another's, and disregards its own advantage, so as to guard the rights of all; thirdly, fortitude, which both in warfare and at home is conspicuous in greatness of mind and distinguishes itself in the strength of the body; fourthly, temperance which preserves the right method and order in all things that we think should either be done or said."[9] St. Ambrose has practically taken over the cardinal virtues of antiquity, added thereto the Christian triad, without sensing that there is a fundamentally different outlook in the two systems. The Christian virtues apparently are conceived as working up from the basis of the four cardinal virtues but not working downward so that the whole scale is radically changed. The whole

7. Cf. More, P.: Hellenistic Philosophies, p. 299.
8. *Plea for the Christians*, IV; cf. XXII.
9. *Duties of the Clergy*, Bk. I, 115.

Gnostic movement was an expression of this intellectualism of the Greeks, and St. Augustine in his struggle against Pelagius was combating the Greek spirit at heart.

The contrast between the two systems becomes apparent also on the question of the unity of virtue. Socrates had declared that knowledge is virtue. Plato, to be sure, had extended the concept of the "virtuous" somewhat, but still retained the emphasis on the intellect. Aristotle followed in his train, as did the Stoics. Virtue according to all of them is really one, and the unifying element is knowledge.[10] The basis of the virtuous life rests finally in the understanding. Hence, for the Stoic the ideal is the wise man. In the light of his understanding and insight all of life is interpreted. In Plato all the virtues were conceived of as forms of knowledge, and so virtue was really one. But according to the Christian view the unifying principle is love. Hence we see here the line which sharply separates the one from the other. Both systems exalt the unity of virtue, but the principle of unification is totally different.

It has been said above that Christianity transfers the emphasis in ethics from the realm of the intellect to that of the will and the emotions. It is with reference to the latter that a very pronounced antithesis appears especially in contrast with Stoicism although Epicureanism took practically the same position. The aim of each of these is to arrive at a state of repose or calm of soul. The Epicurean expressed it in the word ataraxia; the Stoic in apathia. To the Stoic the passions and feelings generally are regarded as an evil which must certainly be suppressed, and if possible eliminated. Because of its glorification of reason it was led to advocate the suppression of the affections, and thereby also expressed its peculiar aloofness from the lot of one's fellow man. The bond of real sympathy was cut because genuine feeling for

10. Stewart, J. A.: Notes on Nic. Ethics, Vol. I, pp. 202-4.
11. Rep, 445c, 519a, Meno 72c etc.

and toward one's neighbor was regarded as beneath the level to which the wise man was to attain. Specifically also with reference to one's own experiences the Stoic maintained that the truly wise man will rise above feeling. Seneca says, "there are certain forerunners of anger, of love, of all those tempests that shake the soul."[12] One should note that love is spoken of as well as anger. And later Aurelius says, "He then is a runaway who is moved by fear, grief, or wrath."[13] This noble emperor had a face that never changed, whether the circumstances called for an expression of joy or sorrow. The ideal was to be surprised and disturbed by nothing, as Horace has said "nil admirari." The ideal of Christianity is not the suppression and elimination of feeling, but the sanctification of them so that they express themselves toward other objects and in another way.

This phase can best be illustrated by the record in the Gospels and the Epistles of Paul. In the life of Jesus there are sufficient evidences of a totally different attitude toward the emotions. For he became angry,[14] and revealed compassion and love,[15] and he manifested joy[16] and sorrow.[17] Throughout the record there is evidence of his tender sympathy with and for suffering humanity. His heart went out to little children and in tenderness of affection embraced them. There is nothing in the perfect man Jesus of that rooting up of all emotion. And the parable he tells of the prodigal son contains an element utterly foreign to the calm lack of emotion of Stoicism. The beautiful words, "when the son was yet a great way off his father saw him, and was moved with compassion, and ran, and fell on his neck, and kissed him,"[18] would certainly reveal weakness and not strength to the Stoic

12. De Ira, III, X, 2.
13. Med. X, 25.
14. Mark 3:5; 10:14; Matt. 9:30; John 11:33, 38.
15. Matt. 20:34; Mark 1:41; Luke 7:13.
16. Luke 10:21.
17. John 11:35; Luke 19:41; Mark 7:34.
18. Luke 15:20.

who would rise above all emotion. Even Aristotle would not have approved such conduct, for the "great-souled" man would ever walk leisurely and not run.

Especially in Paul, the apostle of the gentiles, we find a completely different attitude toward and expression of the emotions. His epistles fairly throb with deep feeling, experiencing it himself, and exhorting others to the manifestation of it toward the brethren. Tenderness and love, considerateness and kindness, these are the ideals for family life between husband and wife, parents and children, brother to brother among the saints of the Church. Such a portrait is not found among the Stoics.[19] It is love which occupies the pivotal place in the virtuous life, and no longer justice or wisdom.[20] Instead of apathy the Christian is exhorted to be fervent in spirit[21] and "to rejoice with them that rejoice and weep with them that weep."[22] But the evidence in Paul is not only that of exhortation. He himself did these very things which he urged upon others. He openly confesses that he weeps for the brethren.[23] He is filled with sorrow and pain[24] and burns within at the causes of stumbling of the brethren.[25] The ideal of apathy was far from his mind.[26] Among the fruits of the spirit are love and joy, — virtues of a positive character which the Stoics did not know.[27]

At this point it is well, therefore, to point out that though there may be some expressions in Paul which apparently are identical with Stoicism, the fundamental outlook and thrust is totally different. The attitude of the ancient was that self-control, moderation, proportion was the ideal, but Paul rises above all that restraint and repression into the fullness of joy

19. Hall, T. C.: History of Christian Ethics, p. 84.
20. Inge, W. Cambridge Biblical Essays, p. 271.
21. Rom. 12:11.
22. Rom. 12:15.
23. Phil. 3:18; II Cor. 2:4; Acts 20:19, 31.
24. Rom. 9:2.
25. II Cor. 11:29.
26. Ramsay, W.: Teaching of Paul, p. 158.
27. Glover, T. R.: World of the New Testament, p. 231.

and peace.   There is no continuity of outlook between the pagan and the Christian point of view but rather a complete break."[28]

We shall now pass on to the triad of Christian virtues, faith, hope, and love   The greatest of these, says Paul, is love. Chief attention will be paid to its character and importance, and little will be said of faith and hope.   The reason does not lie in the lack of importance on the part of these two virtues, but in the fact that in the Christian teaching they acquire a very specific character, and because neither of them was regarded as of particular significance by the ancients. Both of these are very distinctive virtues, the like of which were not of any prominence in pagan antiquity.   It is quite evident why this should be so.   Both faith and hope in the Christian sense stress phases which were lacking among the ancients.   First of all both direct attention to that which is outside of man, namely God, and further emphasize the element of trust in Him, a complete reliance on eternal God for time and eternity.   Just this element of trust is at complete variance with the traditional view of antiquity which based its expectations on the intelligence of man.   It can readily be seen why faith could not possibly be an outstanding activity according to the Greek.   For it postulates the existence of God as a transcendent being, a person of love, truth, righteousness, and holiness.   But we have seen that the Greek ever had a God who was only an intellectual abstraction without person or generally conceived of him only as immanent.   Toward such a god faith cannot exist.   There can be no demand for trust in such a being.   Further the Greek conception of the nature of man also prevents any need of faith and hope. For in so far as man was conceived of as a part of the divine, it would force man to look within and place faith and hope only in himself.

28. Taylor, H. O.: Classical Heritage of Middle Ages. p. 108.

But hope projects itself toward the future. And that future in ancient thought was generally a most vague something, as has been stated above. There was therefore no call for hope with reference to the hereafter, because that very hereafter was denied, or shorn of all brightness. The statement of Paul in the epistle to the Ephesians who are said to be without hope is really a picture of the whole pagan world. Hence, because of their views about God and the future neither faith nor hope could arise. In the Christian view, just because God is so very real, and the future life so very certain, and because man is what he is both faith and hope acquire a position of such supreme importance. The stream of Hebraism has here entered in the channel of Christian thought and completely dominates it.

CHAPTER XVII

Christian and Pagan Ethics

C. *The Greatest of These*

AT THIS POINT we have arrived at the most fundamental and significant element in the Christian outlook. And in this word "love" is contained also the very deep antithesis between the Christian and the pagan view. For the difference is not merely one of addition, of something more, so that love is merely added to the four cardinal virtues of antiquity. But with this word there comes a totally different outlook.[1] The writers of the New Testament realized the difference. All the old things have passed away. For in the classical writers there was reference to Eros (love), and lengthy discussions on it are found.[2] But in the New Testament there is no instance of the use of the word, although agape (love) is used extensively. The reason for the dropping of the word Eros is to be found in that its fundamental meaning, though a kind of love, is one of an opposite character to Christian love. It is idle to lose oneself in general statements about abstractions and thereby forget about the essential difference, e.g., "I never read I Cor. 13 without thinking of the descriptions of the virtues in the Nicomachean Ethics. St. Paul's ethical teaching has quite an Hellenic ring. It is philosophical as resting on a definite principle, viz. our new life in Christ, and it is logical, as classifying virtues and duties according to some intelligible principle."[3] Though the applications of the mean-

---

1. Aleaxander, A.: Christianity and Ethics, p. 196.
2. Cf. Plato's Symposium and Phaedrus.
3. Hicks, E. L.: Studia Biblica, IV, p. 9.

ing of the word agape cannot be kept entirely out of the discussion here, the purpose is to confine it as much as possible to the meaning itself, and later to consider how this conception of love led to different attitudes and conduct in specific relations of the social order.

In the New Testament the statement is specifically made that God is love. This conception is so radically different that the whole atmosphere of human life thereby changes for those who are in communion with God. As He is Love, so they are called to manifest love in such a supreme way that they become worthy representatives of Him. That love is pointed out by Paul as towering above everything else. Therefore it must become central and dominant in one's life. It is first of all a thing of the heart, of emotion and will. Certainly not sentimentality. It is much too virile for that. But the life and deeds of Paul who so magnificently exalts love would hardly give the impression that it is not a matter of emotion. Therefore it seems hardly correct to say that the word for love in the New Testament does not signify any sort of emotion, but a deliberate disposition of the will."[4] It most certainly is a matter of the will, but not a cold, purposeful will, but one burning with zeal for the house of the Lord. The important point is to see that both emotion and will become all important for the virtuous life, and not the intellect alone. "To the quality which he (Paul) calls love he subordinates the reason itself; the life of the mind, though it is neither disregarded nor disowned, becomes a secondary thing."[5]

The pattern of this love is that of God himself. In the Christian it expresses itself in two directions. The law is summarized by Jesus himself in the words: Thou shalt love the Lord thy God with all thy heart, and all thy soul, and with all thy mind. This is the first and great commandment. And the second like unto it, Thou shalt love thy neighbor as thy-

---

4. Gore, C. — *Philosophy of the Good Life,* p. 184.
5. Livingstone, R. W. — *Greek Ideals and Modern Life,* p. 165.

self.[6] The heathen world had put knowledge, wisdom, first; and that a knowledge of oneself. The Hebrew-Christian tradition places the love of God above all else. Such a love begets in the individual all the other virtues as wisdom, courage, temperance. But at the same time it goes out toward one's neighbor. This love rests in God, and therefore gives rest, peace, resoluteness in the soul, but at the same time binds with strong affection to human society.[7] The Christian deals with his fellows benevolently and humanely because he really loves them[8] and does not merely respect them. The point of view of Christian thought is that love gives itself, surrenders self and thinks of self according to the example of the Master who came not to be ministered unto but to minister. But Greek thought always retains something of the self-centered. There is an element of the self-interest in whatever is done to one's fellows.[9]

The point of view is fundamentally quite different between the Greek Eros and the Christian Agape. There is in Greek literature considerable emphasis on Eros. But this Eros cannot be identified with Agape as Dean Inge has done. He writes, "in the Phaedrus as in I Cor. love is the great hierophant of the divine mysteries which forms the link between divinity and humanity.[10]

Love, in the Christian sense, is patterned after the divine love. It is that love which the Christian seeks to imitate. Now, of that love two things can be said. With reference to the object of love, especially man, this love is not caused by his inherent goodness. The Scripture does not in the least present man in that light. God loves him not because he is good, but in spite of his sin and wickedness. The portrayal of that sin is quite terrifying. Man has forsaken God, departed from his

---

6. Matt. 22:37-9.
7. Pfeiderer, O.: Primitive Christianity, Vol. I, p. 409.
8. Cf. Halliday, W. R.: Pagan Background of Early Christianity, p. 135.
9. Earp. T. R.: The Way of the Greeks, p. 218.
10. Inge, W. R.: The Platonic Tradition in English Religious Thought, p. 14.

ways, rejoices in his evil, and hates God who is his creator, and sustains him from moment to moment. But notwithstanding all that, God has loved him with such an intense love that He gave his only-begotten Son even unto death to save man. There is not in man then any thing worthy, because of which God should love him.

Nor again is that love of such a character that it goes out to the object, man, because there is any thought of gain, of acquiring anything. God is in himself perfect, all-sufficient, utterly independent of anything. The love of God is therefore not one that in the least seeks to receive something, but only to give, and to give without measure. The love of God makes the cup to run over. And it does that toward an object totally unworthy of that love and impossible too of making any contribution toward a more perfect state in God. That is the divine Agape.

But the Greek Eros is different. God is love, was entirely new to the Greek. Why should he love? The Gods were perfect, in need of nothing, possessing all. How then could they love? For Eros is expressive of precisely that idea of love, as a striving for something worthy in order thereby to acquire, to gain. He could not conceive of the Gods as giving and, shall we say, spending themselves on unworthy objects. Aristotle has the whole Greek point of view summarized in these words: "He who lives according to reason is the special object of God's love. For if the Gods, as is commonly believed, take thought for our human affairs, we must rationally conclude that they take most pleasure in that which is best and most nearly related to themselves, that is, in our own reason, and that they reward those who live according to reason. It is clear that this is most of all the case with the wise man. Therefore, it is he who is most loved of God."[11] Contrast with this the statement of Paul that God chose the foolish."[12] This

11. *Nic. Ethic,* 1179ª 22ff.
12. I Cor. 1 :27ff.

passage of Aristotle expresses the very core of the Greek conception. Love expresses itself toward that which is worthy, and the thing especially worthy is the intellect. Hence the philosopher is dear to the gods above all others. This conception lies at the bottom of Celsus' violent attacks on the Christian religion. He is scandalized and offended beyond words that sinners are the object of God's love. The Gnostics too carried on the pagan tradition. Salvation was to be attained by the ascent of the soul to God.[13] That is why the gospel was foolishness to the Greeks. And just as the gods could love only that which was worthy, so man in his love toward his fellow could do only the same thing. As God was presented as loving something good in man, so man, when he loved his fellow, did so because of the good in the object of love.

The second characteristic of Eros is that it seeks to gain something. It is the urge, the striving, the intense yearning toward the object of his love for the sake of acquiring, to gain possession. It is the love of desire. "Even when Eros seems to be a desire to give, it is essentially in the last resort, a Will-to-Have."[14] This trait of Eros becomes very clear from a statement in Plato. "Since the gods have all and need nothing, it is impossible to attribute Eros to them."[15] This Eros of acquisition underlies the whole position of ethical thought in the ancient world. In other words, at bottom the ethics of the ancients was egocentric. "Stoicism was essentially self-centered. Its appeal is not to complete self-sacrifice. Self-respect is its driving force rather than love."[16] Christian Agape has something of complete abandonment of self. It teaches self-sacrifice. He who would save his life shall lose it.[17] On the part of God there is condescending love toward poor sinners in order that he may give them eternal life. That is the

---

13. Nygren, A.: Agape and Eros Pt. II Vol. I, p. 184.
14. Idem, p. 134.
15 Symp. 203a.
16. Halliday, W. R.: Pagan Background of Early Christianity p. 136.
17. Mark 8:35.

example and the ideal of love in the Christian also toward his fellow.

Christian love thus has its pattern in the love of God himself as it manifested itself in the way of salvation. It reached out to those who were in no sense worthy of that love, and came to such in their sin. This love is beyond all understanding. The most that we can say is that as far as the objects of the love is concerned it was without cause, was infinite in its expression, and conditioned by nothing outside of God himself. And that same kind of love characterizes Agape in the Christian. There is no thought of the worthiness of the object that we should therefore love him. "The Christian love commandment does not demand love of the fellowman because he is with us equally divine (Stoicism) or because we ought to have 'respect for personality' (Christian liberalism), but because God loves him."[18] Compare with this what Cicero says was taught by the Stoics relative to deeds of kindness: "We should weigh with discrimination the worthiness of the object of our benevolence; we should take into consideration his moral character, his attitude toward us, the intimacy of his relations to us, and our common social ties, as well as the services he has hitherto rendered in our interest."[19]

This Christian concept of love could not but be a revolutionary thing. It affected all human relationships. "This sentiment of love, in which each feels himself responsible for the well-being of the rest, and each is ready to bear his neighbor's burden as his own, was in fact a wholly new phenomenon, the most epoch-making in the ethical history of mankind, something quite distinct from the mere respect for human rights inculcated by the Stoics, or from the friendship of the Epicureans, the aim of which was mere enjoyment from the fellowship of knowledge in the philosophical schools and the legal fellowship of states."[20] "Agape was the reversal of all

18. Niebuhr, R.: Interpretation of Christian Ethics, p. 213.
19. Cicero: De Officiis I, XIV, 45.
20. Pfeiderer, O.: Primitive Christianity, Vol. IV, p. 523.

the values of antiquity."[21]   The teaching that love is the greatest of the virtues stands in direct oppposition to the emphasis of antiquity on wisdom and justice.   "The ancient world, with all its noble and intelligent devotion to truth and justice and the masculine virtues generally, was unable to perceive that the one cure for moral evil is love, and that as Love is necessarily self sacrificing, so vicarious suffering is the deepest and most universal law of Ethics.   This was then and it is now, the leading difference between the wisdom of the world and the Cross."[22]

---

21. Nygren, A.: Agape and Eros, p. 23.
22. Bigg, C.: Christian Platonists, p. 268.

CHAPTER XVIII

Christian and Pagan Ethics

D. *Attitudes Toward Self*

LOVE then is the most basic of the Christian virtues. But there are additional elements in the Christian ethical view which are lacking in pagan antiquity. Among these is the virtue of humility. It follows from the Hebrew-Christian conception of God and of man that humility should play a large part in the pious life. For God is the God of infinite perfection, of power, of truth, of holiness, and of righteousness over against whom man is as nothing. But especially too, since God in his Son descended in love to save man, and thereby humbled himself to the uttermost, man in Christ Jesus is called to manifest that same spirit of humility. The Lord himself repeatedly called attention to the imperative need of this virtue, and Paul frequently praises it and exhorts to the practice of it.

Especially at this point Paul takes a totally different attitude from that of the Stoics. Paul has a sense of complete dependence on God and is therefore humble before Him. There is in him no feeling of self-sufficiency, of independence and strength in himself. Completely alien to the Stoic mind and heart is Paul's expression "When I am weak, then I am strong."[1] The Stoic looked within and trusted to inner strength; Paul looked without and put his trust only in God's power and love.[2] Paul too uses the adjective autarkes (self-

---

1. II Cor. 12:10.
2. Greene, Wm.: Ethics of the New Testament. In Evangelical Quarterly Vol. 111, p. 351.

sufficient) but without the Stoic content. The sufficiency unto all things comes to Paul from God alone. Therefore, although Paul expresses himself in various ways which make one think of Stoicism, the interpretation of these expressions does not accord with the Stoic view.[3]

How could Paul feel independent, self-sufficient over against and all-powerful transcendent God? Greek thought, however, postulated an immanent God and man was part of the divine. But the more the ideal of perfect holiness was before the mind of the saint, the more conscious the Christian would be of his shortcomings with respect to that ideal. The Greek, however, did not see in his gods the ideal of ethical perfection, and hence did not feel humble in comparison with them.

In the Greek conception humility was not thought of as a virtue.[4] The adjective "humble" (tapeinos) is used generally in a bad sense as designating a state of degradation. The Greek emphasized the virtues of agressiveness, of assertiveness over against his fellow citizens; hence there was no place for humility which is the opposite of those characteristics. Th Christian concept of humility has its origin in the relation of man to God, but manifests itself also over against the brethren who one is exhorted to esteem more highly than oneself.[5]

Especially with reference to one's fellows this difference of outlook and attitude is apparent. Throughout Greek thought there is a tendency to cultivate aloofness, independence. The Christian teaching makes much of the body of believers and and the relations which ought to exist between the members. But Greek thought emphasizes the wise individual, who can and does isolate himself from the common experiences, and elevates himself above them and his relations with his fellows. From his lofty height he looks down with a measure of smug self-satisfaction in himself and proud disdain of his fellows.

---

3. Cf. I Cor. 4:8-10; II Cor. 6:10; II Cor. 9:8, 11; Phil. 4:11, 13, 18.
4. Hutton, M.; Greek Point of View, p 51
5. Phil. 2:3.

Diogenes relates that Theodorus held that the wise man, being self-sufficient, has no need of friends.[6] The Christian is exhorted to live in true fellowship of love with the brethren, and above all with the Christ in whom is all power and goodness. Especially, the Stoic had great self-reliance, and felt independent of both men and experiences. The Stoic sought to gain the desired end by self-isolation, while the Christian seeks it by incorporation.[7] The cause of the ancient's feeling as he did was a proud sense of self-sufficiency. He stood above all his fellows, was too big to pay any attention to what they did to him or said of him.[8]

The acme of this proud aloofness and independence is found in Stoicism. The wise man is conscious of his wisdom which elevates him above the masses who have not arrived at that exalted state. He is rich and he is king, living in accord with the divine element in his soul. And as a king, conscious of his power, he repeatedly falls back on the "things within thine own power."[9] "You have but to will a thing and it has happened, the reform has been made."[10]

The emperor wrote: "What richness of leisure doth he gain who has no eye for his neighbor's words or deeds or thoughts but only for his own doings, that they be just and righteous. Verily it is not for the good man to peer about into the blackness of another's heart but to run straight for the goal with never a glance aside."[11] Listen to this passage from Seneca: "In this you may outstrip God, he is exempt from enduring evil, while you are superior to it; scorn poverty; no man lives as poor as he was born. Scorn pain; it will either be relieved or relieve you."[12] Or again, "Most of all, the mind must be withdrawn from external interests into

---

6. Diog, Laert. II. 98.
7. Lightfoot, J. B.: Paul and Seneca. In Apostolic Dissertations p. 290.
8. Nic. Ethics 1124a.
9. Epict. Disc. I, 1, 29; II, 2; IV, 9; Cicero. Tusc. Disp. IV, 31, 65.
10. Epict. IV 9.16.
11. M. Aurelius IV, 18.
12. *De Providentia,* VI, 6.

itself. Let it have confidence in itself, rejoice in itself, let
it admire its own things, let it retire as far as possible from
the things of others and devote itself to itself."[13]   In these
passages there is evident a proud self-sufficiency.   Externals,
both things and people, mean nothing.   What is required is
that man shall exercise his sovereign intelligence and will
which are entirely adequate to take care of all circumstances.
Thus speaks Epictetus: "You must exercise the will — and
the thing is done, it is set right; as on the other hand, only
fall a-nodding and the thing is lost. For from within comes
ruin, and from within comes help."[14]   While Paul teaches
that all his strength comes from God in Christ who dwells in
Him, the Stoic falls back only on himself. There is no need
of outside help. The reservoirs of the human soul alone are
sufficient for all things. While Paul urges unto prayer and
that without ceasing, Seneca says: "What do you want with
prayers? Make yourself happy."[15]

This virtue of humility, so pronounced in the Scripture,
and proclaimed by precept and example, makes abundantly
clear that the Christian and Stoic outlook are not the same.
They are indeed at opposite poles. The explanation is to be
sought in the completely divergent conceptions of God and
man. Naturally the Stoic who believed himself a fragment
of God himself would rely on his own inner power. But the
Christian who recognized himself as nothing, weak and sinful, as an object which was in need of grace, looked not to
self for strength and help, but to God alone who is able to
do all things, and thus save to the uttermost.

Because man was conceived of as a part of the divine and
thus placed high in his own estimation there followed that
other of the characteristic elements in the Christian view were
lacking. Standing out on virtually every page of the New
Testament is the demand for repentance. But because the

---

13. Seneca: *De Tranquilitate* XIV, 2.
14. Disc. IV, 9, 16.
15. Epist. 31, 51.

Greek regarded both God and man in a different light from that which is revealed in both the Old and the New Testaments there is not evident in their literature or life anything approaching the consciousness of sin and the need of repentance which characterize the Scripture. A word therefore about each of these.

Repentance follows from the consciousness of sin. We have seen that the thread running through the Greek and Roman point of view exalted man and hence rested in his self-sufficiency. His ideal of what he was called to be fell far short and therefore he could the more readily become conscious of an approximation to the goal. There is in Plato very little about repentance, in Aristotle nothing at all, and whatever place is given to it among the Stoics was nullified by their proud self-sufficiency. The Stoic did urge on to a careful self-examination, ever again going over what one has said and done with the purpose of making progress. But the very heart of the Christian view, that progress toward the ideal is possible only when the individual has prostrated self, and hence completely denies himself, is entirely lacking. The Greek did not and could not on his fundamental basis understand that he who humbleth himself shall be exalted.

But especially did the Greek not call to repentance because he had no consciousness of sin. Many factors contribute toward the formation of this consciousness. It rests on a specific view of God, of man, and the relation between the two. The God of the Old and New Testaments, infinite in all his perfections, who is perfect truth, righteousness, holiness, all powerful, and infinitely transcending man, revealing himself in his power and majesty, casts man to the earth. His august majesty overwhelms. Therefore Moses declares that no man can see God and live. And when Isaiah sees him in his regal splendor, sitting upon a throne and his train filling the temple, he cries out, "Woe is me, for I am undone. For I am a man of unclean lips, and I dwell in the midst of a people of unclean lips."[16]   Such a conception of God, one who is holy and omnipotent, produces the consciousness of sin.   The loftier the conception of God, the greater will be the depth of man's misery and despair.   That explains the cry from the depth of Paul's soul: "O wretched man that I am! Who will deliver me?"   The essential element in the consciousness of sin is that God is a personal being, perfect in holiness and power.   The sin is against Him.   "Against thee, thee only, have I sinned."[17]

Now consider the fundamental Greek point of view, and it will be perfectly clear why he did not have nor could have a true sense of sin.   The common man still held to the many gods of the Homeric pantheon.   And these, as was stated previously, were not beings who stood before him as the acme of perfect morality.   Hence, there could not be that sense of a thundering holiness manifesting itself against all sin, such as characterized the Old Testament.   The gods of the pantheon stood too close to the ancients to inspire with fear and awe, and their very immorality prevented men from having a sense of sin in their presence.[18]

Again, if the higher conception of the divinity which prevailed among the philosophers is considered, the same holds true.   For their conception of the divinity, though reaching great heights, was merely an abstraction.   God was not a personality, but the rarified form of high thought on the part of the intellect of man.   He was man's own creation, composed of many excellent attributes but not being a living person.   Therefore there could not be that intense consciousness of violating and transgressing his will.

And as for man, little need be added here.   Being, as he supposed, one with the divine, a part of it, how could man possibly have an overwhelming consciousness of sin against a being above and outside of himself?   The Stoic urged men

16. Isaiah 6.
17. Psalm 51.
18. Farnell, L. R.: *Higher Aspects of Greek Religion*, p. 74.

to live in accordance with nature, both that in himself and round about him. On that self and the world men were exhorted to reflect. But that reflection in the presence of which they stood was merely a creature of their own making. The very vital element of a personal being is again lacking.

Thus we find throughout Greek thought the lack of the genuine consciousness of sin, as found in both the Old and the New Testaments. In earlier Greek thought sin was conceived of as something essentially physical. It was not an internal and intensely moral thing. And on the higher level it ever remained only a missing of the mark. One overshot or undershot the mark. But remember that the mark itself was something set up by man, and that by his intellect. In a preceding chapter the intellectualism of the Greeks was discussed rather fully. In accordance with that view sin is merely an error, a mistake of the intellect in perceiving the true and the good.[19] The view of Christianity that sin is due to a perverseness of the will as well as lack of light and understanding is lacking, for the Greek so elevated the intellect that the will receives very scant notice. The two contrasting views have been well stated in these words, "To the Hebrew Paul, sin is not merely an error of the intellect: it is a deterioration and degradation of the will, progressive and illimitable, ending in death. To the Greeks, sin was a failure; to Paul it was a crime."[20] The intellectualism on this point finds full expression in Epictetus, who says, " 'They are thieves,' says someone 'and robbers.' What do you mean by 'thieves and robbers?' They have simply gone astray in questions of good and evil. Ought we, therefore, to be angry with them, or rather pity them? Only show them their error and you will see how quickly they will desist from their mistakes."[21]

Not only was the Greek quite unconscious of sin, but he even disapproved and condemned the consciousness of it.

---

19. Cf. Lightfoot, J. B.: *Apostolic Dissertations*, p. 279.
20. Ramsay, W. M.: *Teaching of Paul*, p. 81.
21. Disc. I, XVIII, 3-4.

There was something wrong with the individual who felt it in a strong degree. And on their basis that is to be understood. In addition to what has been said above, consider the fact that the Deity sought those as his worshippers who were pure and sound. Those who were sinful were under the influence of powers of darkness, and must first recover their health before they could be pleasing to the gods.[22] An interesting parallel is that of the modern who regards him who is deeply conscious of his sins and sinfulness as having an inferiority complex. And when one examines this same modern's views of God and man and compares them with those of the ancients, it is not at all surprising to find the same conclusions. For the modern man too has made his god an abstraction, bereft of personality, and has elevated man to the status of the divine.

The classic example of the Greek who cannot comprehend the confession of sins as the first step toward the true relation with God is Celsus. He ridicules the Christian position in the words: "Let us hear what kind of persons these Christians invite. Everyone, they say, who is a sinner, who is devoid of understanding, who is a child, him will the kingdom of God receive. They assert that God will receive the sinner if he humbles himself on account of his wickedness but that he will not receive the righteous man although he look up to him with virtue from the beginning."[23] How accurately Celsus has described the great difference! The Greek looks up to God "with virtue"; the Christian with none whatever. It is the old story of the publican and the Pharisee!

There is another point of difference, especially between Stoicism and Christianity, on the question of taking one's own life. The Israelite included this in the prohibition "Thou shalt not kill." Human life was regarded as sacred. It was remarked above (Chapter VIII) that, although the Stoic pro-

---

22. Harnack, A.: Expansion of Christianity, Vol. I, p. 125.
23. Origen: Contra Celsum III 59, 62.

claimed a doctrine of Providence, yet many of the leaders committed suicide. In that connection it was pointed out that their view of Providence was inadequate. But those suicides were not deeds done in contravention of their theory. For the leading Stoics taught that suicide is permissible and, one may almost say, obligatory under certain circumstances. The Christian is convinced that "this life and the vocation in it given us by God are a part which we have no right to abandon, but which without murmuring and impatience we must faithfully guard, so long as God himself does not relieve us."[24] But listen to Seneca: "As soon as there are many events in his life that give him trouble and disturb his peace of mind, he (the wise man) sets himself free."[25] Epictetus advises: "Above all things remember that the door is open. Be not more timid than boys at play. As they, when they cease to take pleasure in their games, declare that they will no longer play, so do you, when all things begin to pall on you, retire."[26] Although I give only these two quotations, the conclusion must not be drawn that they are isolated statements. For the fact is that repeatedly it is said in the writings of the Stoics, that there is a way out.[27] And Seneca, Cato, Zeno, Cleanthes all opened the door.

---

24. Bavinck, H.: *Calvin and the Reformation* p. 124.
25. Epist. Mor. LXX. 5.
26. Epictetus: Disc. I XXIV. 20.
27. Cf. Seneca Epist. Mor. XVII, 9; XXX, 2; LVIII, 35: De Providentia II, 12; VI, 7; Epist. Mor. LXX, 5.

CHAPTER XIX

Christian and Pagan Ethics

E. *Attitudes Toward Others*

THE Hellenistic Age was characterized by having a broader and more universal outlook toward humanity. The contributing factors were especially three. There is little doubt that the Mystery religions had an influence. For it is in them that the old religious barriers of race and nationality were broken down. Religion, as practiced in the Mysteries was an individual affair in which women and slaves also could participate.[1] Further, especially the Stoic philosophy taught that there was a common bond between all men, male and female, bond and free. More will be said about this shortly. It would seem though, that the greatest contributing factor was the general political situation. Through the conquests of Alexander the Great the city-state and individual kingdoms were broken up. Men no longer felt themselves bound to a city or to a nation, but became citizens of the world. Through this they felt bound to one another, no longer as citizens but as individuals.

Originally the Greeks especially felt themselves to be a distinctive people. All others were called barbarians. And though it may be true, as Burnet says, that originally this distinction referred only to a difference in language, fact is that in the Golden Age of Greece it had gone very far beyond that.[2] The Greek was very conscious that he was a Greek.

---

1. Gardner, P.: *Religious Experience of Paul,* p. 93.
   Angus, S.: *Religious Quests in the Graeco-Roman World* p. 79.
2. Burnet, J.: *Addresses and Essays,* p. 120.

There was no conception of a common bond between all men. Plato makes a distinction in the Republic which clearly indicates that he did not rise above the common level on ths score. For he will not have it that Greeks war against each other. That must be called "strife"; but as for the barbarians, it shall be war.[8]

Within the city itself the obligations of the Greek citizen were of a limited nature. He owed to his neighbor what was due him as citizen. In other words the concept of justice controlled his actions. And remember that the Greek was ethically self-centered. Those who were weak, poor, sick, oppressed had no claim for special consideration. In the long list of virtues in Aristotle there is none indicating care for and attention to those classes listed above.[4]

During the Hellenistic Age these sharp distinctions between peoples diminished. The Cynics and Stoics both looked beyond the national and racial borders. In Stoic writings there is frequent reference to the brotherhood of all men. So much so that it has been said that Christianity appropriated this idea from Stoicism.[5] But we shall see that the basis on which the "brotherhood" rests is quite different in the latter from that in the former.

What then was the character of Stoic "brotherhood?" It rested on their conception of man and God. The ultimate in all the universe is the Logos. In this both gods and men share. There is a part of the universal Logos in every individual, and that constitutes the bond between all men, as well as between the gods and man. This Logos is the unifying, divine principle in all of life. Because every man has a share in this universal reason he is to be respected by his fellow, but, and that is the weakness of the Stoic conception,

3. Plato's *Republic* — 470c.
4. Rashdall, H: *Conscience and Christ* — p. 85.
5. Case, S. J.: *Evolution of Early Christianity* — p. 280.

this view is intellectualistic. Only the really intelligent belong to the fraternity.[6]

Seneca wrote: "All of us have the same origin, the same source; no man is nobler than another save he who has a more upright character and one better fitted to honorable pursuits."[7] And again, "Man is a sacred thing to man; we are all formed from the same elements, and have the same destiny."[8] Because of this common nature he draws the conclusion, "Nature bids me do good to all mankind — whether slaves or free man, freeborn or freedmen."[9]

These are very noble sentiments. At the same time they reveal an inner contradiction within Stoicism itself. For on the one hand it proclaims a community of being with all men because of which one ought to give himself in service to his fellow. But on the other hand this same Stoicism advocated a proud self-sufficiency in the wise man by which he rises above and away from his fellowmen. Instead of giving himself in a life of service to any and all men in whatever circumstances he finds them, the ideal Stoic isolates himself as far as possible, withdraws into himself in independence of all outward conditions.[10] From that point of isolation and independence he looks down on the masses of humanity who live on such low level.[11] If he does assist, he never forgets his superior position; the help afforded by the wise man is therefore given by a heart filled with proud condescension. How contrary to the Pauline injunction: "Let every man esteem the other more highly than himself."[12]

Christianity too, proclaims a brotherhood in which there is "neither Jew nor Greek, slave or free, male or female."[13]

---

6. Cf. Niebuhr, R.: *An Interpretation of Christian Ethics* — p 49.
7. De Benef. III, 28.
8. Epist. Mor. 95, 33, 52.
9. De Beata Vita XXIV, 3; cf. De Ira II, XXXI, 7.
10. Cf. Inge, W. R.: Outspoken Essays Vol. II, p. 47.
11. M. Aurelius: Med. VI, 10; VII, 62; IX, 27.
12. Phil. 2:31.
13. Gal. 3:28.

But is it identical with the Stoic view? By no means. For the Stoic view rested on nature. The natural man, having a part of the Logos, is bound to all others. But in the Christian conception the brotherhood is in Jesus Christ. Only such as are in Him are members of that fraternity. And membership is based on a supernatural act of regeneration in the heart of man. The "brotherhood" is therefore much less extensive, and of a totally different nature from that which is found among the Stoics.

But this Christian brotherhood, although less extensive than the Stoics, is much more intensive. It is a fraternity of vital relationships. Repeatedly the association of believers is referred to as a body of which the individuals are members.[14] This figure makes the relationship betwen the individuals a living, active thing. It is not an abstraction. The various members are bound to one another, and need one another.[15] Contrast ths with the aloofness and the self-sufficiency of the Stoic wise man, who withdraws himself as far as possible from his fellows! The Christian instead associates with his fellows, acts with them and for them. And the reason for it is two-fold. He needs them no less than they need him! They cannot survive without him, nor can he survive without them. The Christian view therefore, does away at one stroke with the self-centered self-sufficiency of the Stoic.[16]

The motivation of this attitude is love. The Christian feels bound to his fellow believers by the bond of Agape, and actively loves them.[17] Now, that "love" finds its example in the Love of God himself. As God gave himself in love to save men, so the Christian gives himself without thought of self or the worthiness of the object. The love in the heart of the Christian leads him "to spend and be spent," "to minister and not be ministered unto," "to lose his life and thus save it."

14. Rom. 12:4-5; I Cor. 12:27; Eph. 4:4, 16 etc.
15. I Cor. 12:12ff.
16. Cf. Glover: T. R.: *Influence of Christ in the Ancient World,* p. 77.
17. Halliday, W. R.: *Pagan Background of Early Christianity* p. 135.

There are in this Christian attitude two points of interest. The first is that love of one's fellow-man completely eclipses the love of self. It emphasizes abandonment of self, complete self-sacrifice. The "other" stands out, and not the "I."[18] The other point is that exactly through this self-sacrifice the goal is to be reached. The Greek made the man himself the goal. All his actions revolved about himself and returned to him as a boomerang. The goal of self-realization lay in the direction of discovering how all things can contribute toward the man's own comfort and happiness. And that "self" determines the how and the what of one's actions toward his fellowman. But the striking thing in the Christian view is that apparently contradictory position that by the sacrifice of "self" the "self" is destined to reach its goal. "He who loses his life shall save it." This position is at the opposite pole from the pagan view, and of it is said: "His (Paul's) picture of the relation of husband to wife, of child to parent, of fellow-Christian to fellow-Christian, whether bond or free, of citizen even to the oppressive and passing social order, is entirely different from any painted at the heights of Roman Stoicism or amidst the beauties of Platonic ideals."[19] The significance of the two positions is pointed out in these words: "I think it is important to realize that mankind has two different ideals before it; and I do not see how the ideal of Detachment is compatible with the ideal of Love."[20]

This position of "love" is the explanation of the prominence given to benevolence and sympathy. The bond of membership in the same body by which all members suffer if one suffers, naturally leads to efforts to do good and alleviate the suffering. There are sentiments of benevolence especially in later Stoicism. Seneca wrote, "If you imitate the gods, confer benefits even on the unthankful; for the sun rises even on the

18. Cf .Nygren, A.: *Agape and Eros* p. 171.
19. Hall, T. C.: *History of Christian Ethics* p. 84.
20. Bevan, E.: *Stoics and Sceptics*, p. 69.

wicked, and the seas are open to pirates."[21]   But it is difficult
for the Stoic to put such a noble sentiment into practice. For
he stands aloof from the mass of humanity, conscious of his
superiority, proud of his isolation, content with himself in
his sufficiency.   And always there was present the thought
of how these deeds in turn would affect the doer. Cicero
has stated, "We should weigh with discrimination the worthiness of the object of our benevolence; we should take into
consideration his moral character, his attitude toward us, the
intimacy of his relations to us, and our common social ties,
as well as the services he has hitherto rendered in our interest."[22]   This clearly reveals the Stoic attitude in its intellectualism and its self-centeredness.

Because of the real bond between the brethren, Paul does
not hesitate to express his sympathy and pity.[23]   Among the
Stoics who tried to repress the emotions these have no place.
Epictetus declares, "Now another's grief is no concern of
mine, but my own grief is."[24]   And Seneca says that the wise
man will be clement and gentle, but he will not feel pity, for
only old women and girls will be moved by tears.[25]   Thus we
see that what dominates in Stoicism and ancient thought
generally is the stern, independent, indifferent attitude toward
one's neighbor.   All those who are poor, weak, distressed,
sick, in other words all who need sympathy and deserve pity
are passed by.   Christianity here too proclaims an attitude
which was truly revolutionary.[26]

With reference to the attitude toward enemies little need
be said.   It is generally known that the normal attitude in
antiquity was to do evil to one's enemies.   There is even the
refrain to hate him and repay in kind, and double if possible.

---

21. De Benef. IV, 25, 26; cf. VII, 31.
22. De Officiis I, XIV, 45.
23. Cf. Romans 9:1-3; Rom. 12:15; II Cor. 11:28-29.
24. Disc. III 24, 23.
25. Cf. De Clem. II, 5-7.
26. Ottley, R. L.: *Christian Ideas and Ideals* — p. 184.

Plato is the only one who transcends the ordinary Greek feeling.[27] But even here there is a great difference between the
two views. To admonish not to return evil for evil is a long
step forward ethically. However, that is not at all identical
with the Christian precept given by the Lord himself, and
followed by Paul, to do good in return for evil, and so to
overcome evil with good. Not to return evil may be described
as a negative attitude; the Christian view goes on to that
which is definitely positive. There are a number of bits of
evidence to indicate that among the Stoics especially there
were those who had risen to the former height.[28] In one of
these passages Epictetus says, "First consider what injury is,
and call to mind what you have heard the philosophers say,
for if the good lies in moral purpose, and the evil likewise in
moral purpose, see if what you are saying does not come to
something like this. 'Since so-and-so has injured himself
by doing me some wrong, shall I not injure myself by doing
him some wrong?' "[29]

And what about the inner attitude toward the wrong doer?
Shall he be whole-heartedly forgiven? Thus says Christianity, and therefore goes on to teach overcoming the evil with
the good.[30] But one would not expect that attitude of for-
giveness among the Stoics. Seneca says, "There is no reason
why thou shouldest be angry; pardon them; they are all
mad."[31] His position is not one of understanding and for-
giving love toward the offender. Rather from his height he
looks down in contempt on those who have thus tried to injure him. It has been correctly observed that this in no way
compares with the "Father, forgive them" of the Cross.[32]

---

27. Shorey, P.: "Greek Religion" in Sneath's *Evolution of Ethics* p. 257
28. Epictetus: Disc. I. 13, 2; I. 18, 9; II. 10. 24; IV. 1. 120; M. Aurelius: Med III. 11; VI. 6; VII. 26; X. 30.
29. Disc. II, X, 24-26.
30. Rom. 12:21.
31. De Benef. V, 17.
32. Hicks, E.: *Traces of Greek Philosophy and Roman Law in the N. T.*
p. 113.

For the one is the expression of divine love, the other of subtle egotism, by which the proud wise man refuses even to recognize that the deed touches his unruffled self.

With reference to the question of slavery and the treatment of slaves there is progress in the history of Greek thought. In the classical period it was generally justified. One could expect nothing else in view of the sharp distinction which was made between Greek and barbarian. But even then there are voices raised against it as that of Euripides. Plato appears silently to abolish it, since there are no slaves in his Utopia. But Aristotle, as is well known, justified the institution.[33] The Cynics and Stoics condemned it, the latter because of the common nature of all men. Thus Seneca writes: "Kindly remember that he whom you call your slave sprang from the same stock, is smiled upon by the same skies, and on equal terms with yourself breathes, lives, and dies."[34]

Though the New Testament Scripture does not explicitly condemn slavery, the whole thrust of its teaching is against the institution. In Christ there is neither bond or free, and the saints are admonished to love one another, and in practice the converted slaves were regarded as brothers and sisters in the full sense of the terms and their personalities were esteemed just as highly as the freemen.[35]

---

33. Cf. Pol. Bk. I. chaps. IV-VII.
34. Epist. Mor. XLVII. 10.
35. Cf. Harnack, A.: Expansion of Christianity Vol. I. p. 208-210.

CHAPTER XX

Epilogue

The object of these remarks is not to make an abstract of the whole territory covered in the preceding pages but rather to formulate a few general conclusions. On the basis of the evidence there is no single formula which will adequately describe all the phenomena. The material has appeared much too complex for such a simple characterization. Hence we find something like the following statements necessary to a right description of the many phases of ancient life as compared with the Christian view.

First, some of the cardinal Christian teachings find no place in the views of the ancient Greeks and Romans. They are entirely absent from their view of life. This, however, is a small number.

Second, there are also phases of life or views with reference to such phases quite directly contradictory to the view of Christianity. This antithetical view was strongly felt by some of the apologists and Fathers of the church. The instances of such direct opposition are also comparatively few.

Finally, there is a large number of points of view in which the same subject is treated. In these instances there is often an approach to the Christian view, and in some cases one can find a real similarity in expression. Taken by themselves, removed from their general background, they appear to teach the same thing. However, a careful investigation into the real meaning of such apparently similar expressions in view of other teachings and the general background has not revealed identity but divergence or opposition or deficiency. It appears therefore that formally there is a real approach to identity but materially there is not. For either the approach contains contradictory elements or it falls short. In every case there has appeared a unique element in the Christian view. There is indeed a special revelation.

191

Bibliography

Adam, J. *Religious Teachers of Greece.* Edinburgh: T & T Clark, 1909.
Ambrose, St. *Post-Nicene Fathers.*
Allies, T. W. *The Formation of Christendom.* London: Burns & Coates.
Alexander, A. *Christianity and Ethics.* N. Y. Charles Scribner's Sons, 1922.
Anderson, Scott; *Saint Paul, The Man and the Teacher.* Cambridge, 1936.
Andrews, M. E. *The Ethical Teaching of Paul. Chapel Hills U. of N. C.,* 1934. *Paul, Philo, and the Intellectuals.* J. B. Lit. Vol. LIII, 1934.
Angus, S. *The Environment of Early Christianity.* N. Y.: Charles Scribner's Sons, 1921. *The Mystery Religions and Christianity.* N.Y.: Charles Scribner's Sons, 1925. *The Religious Quests of the Graeco-Roman World.* N. Y.: Charles Scribner's Sons, 1929.
Ante-Nicene Christian Library, A. Roberts and J. Donaldson, Edinburgh; T & T. Clark, 1867-1872.
Phenomena, Aratus. Loeb Library.
Arnold, E. V. *Roman Stoicism.* Cambridge, 1911.
Arnold, M. *Culture and Anarchy.* N. Y. Macmillan, 1897.
Aristotle, Loeb Library.
Asch, S. *The Apostle.* N. Y.: Putnam's, 1943.
Athenagoras, *Ante-Nicene Christian Library.*
Augustine, St. *Post-Nicene Fathers.* P. Schaff. Edinburgh, 1890-1908.
Aurelius, M. *Meditations.* Loeb Library.

Barbour, C. E. *Sin and the New Psychology.* Chicago: Abingdon Press, 1930.
Bauer, A. *Com Gniechentum zum Christentum.* Leipzig: Quelle & Myer, 1910.
Bavinck, H. *Calvin and the Reformation.* Chicago: F. H. Revell, 1909; *Het Ryk Gods, In Kennis en Leven.* Kampen, J. H. Kok: 1922.
Beryaev, N. *The Meaning of History.* N. Y.: Charles Scribner's Sons, 1936.
Bevan, E. *Hellenism and Christianity.* London: Allen & Unwin, 1921; *Stoics and Sceptics.* London: Clarendon Press, 1913.
Bigg, C. *The Christian Platonists of Alexandria.* N. Y.; Oxford, 1886.
Bousset, W. *Kurios Christos.* Gottingen: Vanden hoeck & Ruprecht, 1921.
Box, G. H. *Early Christianity and the Hellenic World.* Expositor, 1924.
Bultmann, R. *Der Stil der paulinischenPredigt und die kynisch-stoische Diatribe.* Gottingen: Vandenhoeck & Ruprecht, 1910.
Burnet, J. B. *Essays anl Addresses.* N. Y.; Macmillan, 1930.
De Witt Burton, E. *Spirit, Soul and Flesh.* Chicago: U. of C., 1918.
Bury, J. B. *The Hellenistic Age.* Cambridge, 1923.
Buswell, J. *Relation of Christianity to Ancient Religions.* Bib. Sacra, 1924.
Butcher, S. H. *Some Aspects of the Greek Genius.* London: Macmillan, 1916; *Originality of Greece.* London: Macmillan, 1920.

Cadoux, C. J. *The Early Church and the World.* Edinburgh: T & T. Clark, 1925.

Caird, E. *Evolution of Theology in Greek Philosophy.* Glasgow: J. Maclehose & Sons, 1904.

Calvin, J. *Commentaries.* Grand Rapids: Eerdmans, 1948-1950.

Campbell, L. *Religion of Greek Literature.* N. Y.: Longmans Green, 1898.

Carpenter, J. E. *Phases of Early Christianity.* N. Y.: Putnam's Sons, 1916.

Carter, J. B. *The Religion of Numa.* London: Macmillan, 1906; *The Religious Life of Ancient Rome.* Boston: Houghton Mifflin, 1911.

Carus, P. *The Pleroma: An Essay on the Origin of Early Christianity.* Chicago: Open Court, 1909.

Case, S. J. *The Evolution of Early Christianity.* Chicago: U. of C., 1914; *Experience with the Supernatural in Early Christian Times.* N. Y. Century, 1929; *The Social Origins of Christianity.* Chicago: U. of C., 1923; *Studies in Early Christianity.* N. Y.: Century, 1928.

Charles, R. H. *Apocrypha and Pseudepigrapha.* Oxford, 1913.

Cicero. Loeb Library.

Cleanthes, *Hymns to Zeus,* in Von Arnim. Stoicorum Veterem Fragmenta.

Clemen, C. *Primitive Christianity and Its Non-Jewish Sources.* Edinburgh: T & T Clark, 1912.

Cumont, F. *The Oriental Religions in Roman Paganism.* Chicago: Open Court, 1911.

Deissmann, A. *Light from the Ancient East.* N. Y.: George Doran, 1927; *St. Paul — A Study in Social and Religious History.* N. Y.: Hodder & Stoughton, 1912.

Demos, R. *The Philosophy of Plato.* N. Y.: Charles Scribner's Sons, 1939.

Dill, S. *Roman Society from Nero to Marcus Aurelius.* N. Y.: Macmillan, 1925.

Diogenes Laertius, Loeb Library.

Dio Chrysostom, Loeb Library.

Dodd, C. H. *The Bible and the Greeks.* London: Hodder & Stoughton, 1935.

Döllinger, J. J. *The Gentile and the Jew.* London: Longmans Green, 1862.

Dorsey, G. A. *Man's Own Show.* N. Y.: Harper's. 1931.

Drummond, J. *Philo Judaeus.* London: Williams & Norgate, 1888.

DuBose, W. P. *The Gospel in the Gospels.* N. Y.: Longmans Green, 1923.

Duchesne, L. *The Early History of the Christian Church.* N. Y.: Longmans Green, 1923.

Earp, F. R. *The Way of the Greeks.* London: Oxford, 1929.

Easton, B. S. *The Pauline Theology and Hellenism.* A. J. Theol. 21.

Edman, I. *The Mind of Paul.* N. Y.: Henry Holt, 1935.

Enslin, M. S. *The Ethics of Paul.* N. Y.: Harper, 1930

Epictetus, Loeb Library.

Fairweather, W. *Jesus and the Greeks,* Edinburgh: T & T. Clark, 1924; *The Background of the Epistles.* N. Y.: Charles Scribner's Sons, 1935.

Farnell, L. R. *The Higher Aspects of Greek Religion.* N. Y.: Charles Scribner's Sons, 1912.

Farrer, J. A. *Paganism and Christianity.* London: A & C Black, 1891.

Faulkner, J. A. *The Greek and the Fulness of Time.* Bib. Rev. 1932.

Ferguson, W. S. *Hellenistic Athens*. N. Y.: Macmillan, 1911.
Fisher, G. P. *Supernatural Origin of Christianity*. N. Y.: Charles Scribner's Sons, 1890.
Foakes F. J.-Jackson and Kirsopp-Lake, *The Beginnings of Christianity*. London: Macmillan, 1920.

Gardner, P. *The Religious Experience of Paul*. Putnam's Sons, 1913.
Geesink, W. *Gereformeerde Ethiek*. Kampen: J. H. Kok, 1931.
Gilbert, G. H. *Greek Thought in the New Testament*. N. Y.: Macmillan, 1928.
Glover, T. R. *The Conflict of Religions in the Early Roman Empire*. London: Methuen, 1920; *The Influence of Christ in the Ancient World*. Cambridge: Yale U., 1929; *Paul of Tarsus*. N. Y.: G. H. Doran, 1925; *The World of the New Testament*. N. Y.: Macmillan, 1931.
Gore C. *The Philosophy of the Good Life*. N. Y.: Charles Scribner's Sons, 1930.
Grant A. *The Ancient Stoics, in Ethics of Aristotle*. London: Longmans Green, 1874.
Greene, Wm. *Ethics of the New Testament*. Evang. Quart. III.

Hack, R. K. *God in Greek Philosophy to the Time of Socrates*. Princeton: Un. Press, 1931.
Hall T. C. *History of Ethics Within Organized Christianity*. N. Y.: Charles Scribner's Sons, 1910.
Halliday, W. R. *The Pagan Background of Early Christianity*. London: Hodder & Stoughton, 1925; *Lectures on the History of Roman Religon from Numa to Augustus*. Liverpool, 1923.
Harnack, A. *Expansion of Christianity in the First Three Centuries*. N. Y.: Putnam's Sons, 1904; *History of Dogma*.
Harris, J. R. *The Origin of the Prologue to St. John's Gospel*. Cambridge: Un. Press, 1917.
Harrison, Jane, *Prolegomena to the Study of Greek Religion*. Cambridge, 1922.
Hasler F. *Verhältniss der heidnischen und christlichen Ethik* München: G. Franz, 1866.
Hatch, E. *The Influence of Greek Ideas and Usages on the Christian Church*. London: Williams & Norgate, 1892.
Hatch, W. H. *The Pauline Idea of Faith*. Cambridge: Harvard Un. Press, 1917.
Headlam, A. C. *St. Paul and Christianity*. N. Y.: Longmans Green, 1913.
Heinrici, D. C. F. *Hellenismus und Christentum*. Berlin: Edwin Runge, 1909.
Hesiod, Loeb Library.
Hicks, E. *Traces of Greek Philosophy and Roman Law in the New Testament*. N. Y.: E. & J. Young, 1896.
Hicks, R. D. *Stoic and Epicurean*. N. Y.: Charles Scribner's Sons, 1910.
Hippolytus, *Ante-Nicene Christian Library*.
Hutton, M. *The Greek Point of View*. N. Y.: George Doran.

Inge, Wm. *Christian Ethics and Modern Problems*. N. Y.: Putnam's Sons, 1910; *The Platonic Tradition in English Religious Thought*. N. Y.: Longmans Green, 1926; *Outspoken Essays* Vol. II.
Irenaeus, *Ante-Nicene Christian Library*.

James, E. O. *In the Fulness of Time*. London: S. P. C. K., 1935.
Jevons, F. B. *Hellenism and Christianity*. Harv. Theol. Rev., 1908.
Jones, M. *Hellenistic World Behind the New Testament*. Expositor, 1921; *St. Paul the Orator*. London: Hodder & Stoughton, 1910.
Justin Martyr, *Ante-Nicene Christian Library*.

Kennedy, H. A. *Philo's Contribution to Religion*. London: Hodder & Stoughton, 1919; *St. Paul and the Mystery Religions*. N. Y.: Hodder & Stoughton, 1913.
Knopf, R. *Paul and Hellenism*. Amer. Jour. of Theol., 1914.
Knox, W. *St. Paul and the Church of the Gentiles*. Cambridge: Un. Press, 1939.

Lactantius, *Ante-Nicene Christian Library*.
Lecky, W. E. *History of European Morals*. N. Y.: D. Appleton, 1897.
Legge, F. *Forerunners and Rivals of Christainity*. Cambridge: Un. Press, 1915.
Lightfoot, J. B. *St. Paul and Seneca,* In Dissertations on the Apostolic Age. N. Y.: Macmillan, 1892.
Lindsay, T. M. *The Church and Its Ministry in the Early Centuries*. London: Hodder & Stoughton, 1902.
Livingstone, R. W. *Greek Ideals and Modern Life*. Oxford: Clarendon Press, 1935; *The Greek Genius and Its Meaning to Us*. London: Oxford, 1924.
Lucretius, Loeb Library.
Luthardt, *Geschichte der Christlichen Ethik*. Leipzig: Dorffling & Franke, 1888.

Macchiono, V. D. *From Orpheus to Paul*. N. Y.: Henry Holt, 1930.
Macgregor, G. H. C. & Purdy, A. C. *Jew and Greek, Tutors unto Christ*. N. Y.: Charles Scribner's Sons, 1936.
Machen, J. G. *The Origin of Paul's Religion*. Grand Rapids: Eerdmans, 1947.
Macmurray, J. *The Clue to History*. N. Y.: Harper's, 1939.
McClure, M. J. *Greek Conception of Nature*. Phil. Rev., 1934.
McGiffeet, A. C. *The Apostolic Age*. N. Y.: Charles Scribner's Sons, 1897.
McNeill J. T. et al., *Environmental Factors in Christian History*. Chicago: U. of C., 1939.
Means, S. *Faith*. N. Y.: Macmillan, 1933.
Mercier, L. J. *The Challenge of Humanism*. N. Y.: Oxford, 1933.
Merrill, E. T. *Essays on Early Christianity*. London: Macmillan, 1924.
Minar, E. L. *The Logos of Heracleitus*. Class. Phil., 1939.
Moffatt, J. *Love in the New Testament*. N. Y.: R. Smith, 1930.
Moore, C. H. *Religious Thought of the Greeks*. Cambridge: Harvard Press, 1916.

More, P. E. *Hellenistic Philosophies.* Princeton: Un. Press, 1923.
Murray, G. *Five Stages of Greek Religion.* N. Y.: Columbia Un. Press, 1925.

Neander, A. *Relation of Grecian and Christian Ethics.* Bib. Sac., 10.
Niebuhr, R. *An Interpretation of Christian Ethics.* N. Y.: Harper, 1935.
Nilsson, M. P. *A History of Greek Religion.* N. Y.: Oxford, 1925
Nock, A. D. *Early Gentile Christianity and Its Hellenistic Background* in *Essays on the Trinity and the Incarnation.* London: Longmans Green, 1928.
Norton, F. O. *The Rise of Christianity.* Chicago: U. of C., 1924.
Nygren, A. *Agape and Eros.* London: SP. C.K., 1932, 1938, 1939.

Origen, *Ante-Nicene Christian Library.*
Ottley, R. L. *Christian Ideas and Ideals.* N. Y.: Longmans Green, 1916
Pfleiderer, O. *Christian Origins.* N. Y.: B. Huebsch, 1906; *Primitive Christianity.* N. Y.: Putnam's Sons, 1906.
Philo, Loeb Library.
Pickman, E. M. *The Mind of Latin Christendom.* N. Y.: Oxford, 1937.
Plato, Loeb Library.
Price, E. J. Paul and Plato. Hibbert Journal 16.

Ramsay, Wm. *The Church and the Roman Empire.* N. Y.: Putnam's Sons, 1912; *The Cities of St. Paul.* N. Y.: George Doran, 1907; *St. Paul the Traveller and the Roman Citizen.* N. Y.: Putnam's Sons, 1896.
Rashdall, Hastings, *Conscience and Christ.* N. Y.: Charles Scribner's Sons, 1916.
Rendall, G. H. *Immanence, Stoic and Christian.* Harvard Theol., Rev. 14.
Rohde, E. *Psyche.* N. Y.: Harcourt, Brace, 1925.
Rose, C. P. *Antecedents of Christianity.* London: Williams & Norgate, 1925.
Ross, D. M. *The Spiritual Genius of St. Paul.* N .Y.: George Doran.

Schmidt, C. *Social Results of Early Christianity.* London: Wm. Isbister, 1889.
Scott, E. F. *The Gospel and Its Tributaries.* N. Y.: Charles Scribner's Sons, 1930.
Scullard, H. H. *The Ethics of the Gospel and the Ethics of Nature.* N. Y.: Doubleday Doran, 1928.
Seneca, Loeb Library.
Shorey P. *Ethics of the Greek Religion,* in E. H. Sneath *Evolution of Ethics.* New Haven: Yale Un. Press, 1927.
Sihler, E. G. *From Augustus to Augustine.* Cambridge: Un. Press, 1923; *Paul and Seneca.* Bib Rev, 1927.
Spence, H. D. *Early Christianity and Paganism.* N. Y.: E. P. Dutton, 1902.
Stewart, J. A. *Notes on Nic Ethics.* Oxford: Un Press, 1892.

Tarn, W. W. *Hellenistic Civilization*. London: E. Arnold, 1930.

Tatian, *Ante-Nicene Christian Library*.

Taylor, A. E. *The Faith of a Moralist*. London: Macmillan, 1930; *Plato, The Man and His Work*. N. Y.: The Dial Press, 1936.

Taylor, H. O. *Classical Heritage of the Middle Ages*. N. Y.: Macmillan, 1911.

Tertullian, *Ante-Nicene Christian Library*.

Theophilus, *Ante-Nicene Christian Library*.

Tucker, T. G. *Life in the Roman World of Nero and St. Paul*. N. Y.: Macmillan, 1917.

Uhlhorn, G. *Conflict of Christianity with Heathenism*. N. Y.: Charles Scribner's Sons, 1879.

Walton, F. E. *Development of the Logos Doctrine in Greek and Hebrew Thought*. Bristol: J. Wright and Sons, 1911.

Warde Fowler, W. *The Religious Experience of the Roman People*. London: Macmillan, 1911; *Social Life at Rome in the Age of Cicero*. N. Y.: Macmillan, 1916.

Warfield, B. *The Terminology of Love in the New Testament*. Princeton Theol. Rev., 1918.

Weigall, A. *The Paganism in Our Christianity*. N. Y.: Putnam's, 1930.

Weinel, H. *St. Paul, the Man and His Work*. N. Y.: Putman's 1906.

Weiss, J. *The History of Primitive Christianity*. N. Y.: Wilson-Erickson, 1937.

Wendland, P. *Die Hellenistisch-romische Kultur*. Tubingen: J. C. Mohr, 1912.

Wenley, R. M. *The Preparation for Christianity*. N. Y.: 1898.

Whittaker, T. *The Origins of Christianity*. London: Watts & Co., 1909.

Wielenga, G. *Paulus*, Kampen: J. H. Kok, 1917.

Wilson, T. *St. Paul and Paganism*. Edinburgh: T & T Clark, 1927.

Zielinski, T. *The Religion of Ancient Greece*. N. Y.: Oxford, 1926.